I0137265

PRAISE FOR PARENTING CONNECTION

"The most important component of living a long, happy, and healthy life is human connection. It is the development of this connection early in life that sets the framework for such connections in the future. In this thoroughly researched and practical book, one is given the tools to develop a caring and compassionate relationship between parent and child and set the stage for your child's success in the future. I highly recommend that every parent read *Parenting Connection*."

—James R. Doty, M.D.
New York Times and International Bestselling Author of *Into the Magic Shop: A Neurosurgeon's Question to Discover the Mysteries of the Brain and the Secrets of the Heart*

"Trust is the foundation for any successful relationship. To achieve trust, one has to make sincere and holistic connections. These connections deepen when one understands the emotions of others, especially when one cannot articulate their feelings. Ms. Terpetska leverages her research and experience working with children to better inform parents about the emotional challenges their child is battling. The lessons and guidance are invaluable if you truly want to improve your relationship with your child. I highly recommend *Parenting Connection.*"

—Michael H. Glasheen
M.A. in Organizational Leadership

———

"If you could read one book on parenting children without conflict, this book should be at the top of your list. Albina Terpetska helps to remove the struggle from parenting while showing a clear and precise way to build a true connection with children. Albina combines cutting edge research with her experiences and best practices as both an educator and a family coach. I highly recommend this book and the strategies within."

—Daryl Moore
Author of *Abandoned and Shattered: Surviving and Thriving After the Pain of a Breakup You Didn't Want*

———

"Being a parent is challenging under any circumstances, so if you seek to become a more effective parent, make *Parenting Connection* a part of your library today. I have learned many useful strategies and techniques for enhancing and deepening the precious relationship I have with my two children.

Albina Terpetska is a first-class professional with strong insights. Her guidance will be beneficial for parents seeking to improve or heal the way they communicate with their children. I enjoyed reading this comprehensive parenting guide, and I recommend this book enthusiastically and without reservation."

—Robert San Luis
Author of #1 International Bestselling Author of *Wealth Without Wall Street: Seven Keys to an Early Retirement*

"*Parenting Connection* offers both the mindset and strategies needed to create the parent-child relationship you are looking for, whether you're first starting out or need to 'fix' what's happening. This book will make a great difference in the relationship you have with your child. If you're a growth-mindset oriented person, these techniques will transform your relationship with your child, and, as a result, help your child become emotionally aware as well."

—Gregg Korrol
Principal, results coach, and author of *The Gifted Storyteller: The Power is in the Story You Tell*

"Albina Terpetska's book will help you to reprogram your relationship with your children from the inside out. Parenting does not have to be a stressful experience. *Parenting Connection* will guide you to create a stronger connection with your children even during busy or chaotic times."

—Dr. Brian P. Ramos
Author of *The Art of Stress-Free Living: Reprogram your Life from the Inside Out*

"As a father of four, I wish I had Albina's straight-forward, easy-to-apply, and insightful book *Parenting Connection* when my now-adult children were younger. I am sure my four children would agree! Albina's extensive knowledge and passionate dedication to helping parents with the daunting task of raising loving, confident children is apparent in the vast amount of information found throughout this book. For any parent frustrated with how to best raise their children, this is definitely worth your time and consideration!"

—Jose Diaz
Tony Robbins's trainer, life coach

"I have witnessed a first-hand account of Ms. Terpetska's words put into action! I accompanied her on several home visits where I was astonished at her ability to bridge relationships with parents and educators. I was in amazement watching her deal with students who struggled with their emotions when trying to communicate their feelings in a positive manner. Ms. Terpetska's community engagement goes beyond words on the pages of this extraordinary map in building stronger bonds between parents and their children.

My children are all adults, yet the words on the pages remind me of the importance of my daily interaction with them. No matter how old children get, dealing with your emotions in a viable way is important when thriving in day-to-day living in all aspects of one's life. I recommend all parents read this guide in strengthening a bond and engaging in positive interaction that can be passed down from generation to generation."

—Letta S. Mason
MA, M.Ed

"Albina Terpetska guides you through the steps you need to take to have the parent-child relationship you want by dispelling the common misconceptions and beliefs that prevent too many parents from creating their dream relationships with their children. At the end of this book, you'll have all of the answers."

—Christian Rodwell
Author of *Sack Your Boss: The Ultimate Guide To Escape Your 9-5*

"You look into your child's eyes and see them looking back into yours, and you can feel not just a desire, but a deep ache to connect. But then you don't because you don't know what to say or even listen for. Through reading this wonderful book, you will correct all that, so you will never have the very sad and avoidable story at the end of your lives of parents and children who deeply loved, but never knew each other."

—Mark Goulston, M.D.
Author of *Just Listen: Discover the Secret to Getting Through to Absolutely Anyone*

PARENTING CONNECTION

CREATE THE PARENT-CHILD RELATIONSHIP YOU AND YOUR CHILD DESERVE

ALBINA TERPETSKA

Lasting Press

Copyright © 2020 Albina Terpetska

All Rights Reserved. No part of this publication may be reproduced or transmitted in any form or by any means, mechanical or electronic, including photocopying and recording, or by any information storage and retrieval system, without permission in writing from the author or publisher (except by a reviewer, who may quote brief passages in a review).

Disclaimer: The Publisher and the Author make no representations or warranties concerning the accuracy or completeness of the contents of this work and expressly disclaim all warranties of fitness for a particular purpose. No warranty may be created or extended by sales or promotional materials. The advice and strategies contained herein may not be suitable for every situation. This work is sold with the understanding that the Publisher is not engaged in rendering legal or other professional services. If professional assistance is required, the services of a competent professional person should be sought. Neither the Publisher nor the Author shall be liable for damages arising therefrom. The fact that an organization or website is referred to in this work as a citation and/or potential source of further information does not mean that the Author or the Publisher endorses the information the organization or website may provide or recommendations it may make. Further, readers should be aware that internet websites listed in this work may have changed or disappeared between when this work was written and when it is read.

Disclaimer: The cases and stories in this book have had details changed to preserve privacy, or clients have permitted their names to be used.

ISBN: 978-1-949696-13-4 (epub)

ISBN: 978-1-949696-14-1 (paperback)

Published by:

Lasting Press

615 NW 2nd Ave #915

Canby, OR 97013

Project Management: Rory Carruthers Marketing

Cover and Interior Design: Rory Carruthers Marketing

www.RoryCarruthers.com

For more information about Albina Terpetska or to book her for your next event, speaking engagement, podcast, or media interview, please visit: www.albinspire.com

DEDICATION

To my mom, Svitlana, and my sister, Violetta, for giving me the gift of experiencing connection at its deepest levels and in the most meaningful ways.

DOWNLOAD THE FREE PRINTABLE COMPANION WORKBOOK!

To help you implement what you will learn in *Parenting Connection,* I am giving you the companion workbook for free!

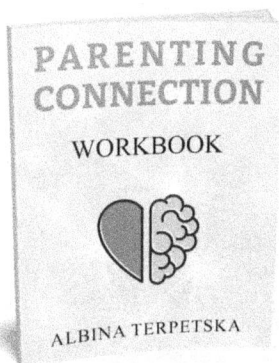

**Download your copy of the workbook at:
www.albinspire.com/workbook**

CONTENTS

PREFACE

I am delighted and honored that you have picked up *Parenting Connection: Create the Parent-Child Relationship You and Your Child Deserve* in search of answers to your questions on parenting. In this book, I will guide you through the maze of obstacles and confusion to discover how you can have the parent-child relationship you have always dreamt of.

Parent-child relationships are incredibly important and powerfully impact our entire lives. My earnest desire is to help parents and children eliminate unnecessary emotional suffering from their lives and create the relationships they deserve by fully connecting with one another. *Parenting Connection* is the book that I wish I had when I began working with children and wish my parents had when I was a child. The insights in this book will help you realize that you are already able to give your child the foundation he needs—a fully connected parent-child relationship—to create the life he wants.

In this book, I do not teach you how to become a better parent. Teaching you how to become a better parent would mean teaching you how to love, care about, and want what's best for your child even more than you already do. You and I both know that you already love, care about, and want what's best for your child. You are already giving your child what matters the most: your wisdom, heart, and soul.

Teaching you how to become a better parent would imply that you are "not good enough," which couldn't be farther from the truth. What does it even mean "to be good enough"? I wish society would stop telling you that you need to become a better parent while giving you all the reasons you are not good enough. Your goodness is unmeasurable and unquestionable. Just like your child, you are incomparable, unique, and special.

Instead, in this book, I share the lessons I have learned in my personal and professional life to empower you with the skills you need to use the resources you already have more purposefully and consciously in ways that better serve you and your child.

The Components of Connected Parenting

The book is divided into three parts. Throughout each part, I have chosen to alternate masculine and feminine pronouns. I hope this book will be equally useful to parents of both daughters and sons.

In Part I, *The Foundation for a Fully Connected Parent-Child Relationship,* you are empowered with a deep understanding of how adult and child brains function so that you can avoid the harmful mistakes that many parents make. By the end of Part I, you will also have a clear understanding of your own needs and your child's needs and know how to distinguish between destructive and constructive ways of meeting those needs.

In Part II, *The Parenting Success Formula,* you learn how to use the Parenting Success Formula that I share with my private coaching clients so that you can connect with your child by changing your actions, and in turn, those of your child to achieve results that benefit both of you. I also reveal the life-changing beliefs that help you build a fully connected relationship with your child.

In Part III, *Empowering Yourself and Your Child with Emotional Mastery,* I introduce the ten steps that you can use to help your child experience and productively use his emotions. I break down each step and provide you with vivid examples of each so that you can successfully implement them with your child. In this part, the lessons you learn will prevent you from making the common mistakes that most parents make when attempting to help their child with his emotions. You will learn how to teach your child to connect with and trust himself, as well as preserve your child's feelings of self-worth and lovability while maintaining a meaningful connection between the two of you. In addition, you learn practical ways to stay self-connected, even in the most challenging parenting situations.

The Beginning of Your New Parenting Journey

Because of the useful and practical insights I share in the book, you may be tempted to read the entire book as quickly as possible. This book introduces complex concepts and is packed with wisdom, effective strategies, and profound insights that you may need time and space to reflect on and internalize. I encourage you to read no more than one chapter at a time and then reflect on it, take notes, and give yourself time to practice implementing what you learned rather than quickly consuming the information. To get the most benefit from this book, I recommend using the corresponding exercises found in the complimentary *Parenting Connection Workbook.* Go now to albinspire.com/workbook to download your free copy!

With this book, the power to change the entire trajectory of your life, your child's life, and the lives of future generations lies in your hands. You and your child CAN create the parent-child relationship you both deserve, regardless of what it feels and looks like right now. I want to encourage you to believe in your child and yourself and inspire you to begin today. I will be here for you, walking along with you on your journey, to support you in creating the parent-child relationship you both deserve.

INTRODUCTION: MY QUEST TO DISCOVER WHAT WORKS

"If only my child would listen..." Exhausted from dealing with daily tantrums, backtalk, rolled eyes, fighting, name-calling, and other types of disrespectful and sometimes even violent behavior, many parents believe that their child's behavior is the ultimate cause of all the drama and emotional suffering in their parent-child relationship.

They are convinced that a fulfilling parent-child relationship could be possible if only their child would behave. Focused on finding a solution for how to "fix" their child's behavior, parents spend countless hours looking for easily-available tips and tricks from well-intended friends and parenting sites on how to get their child to listen. Some of those approaches may work temporarily, but they never last and often result in even more emotional suffering. Hopeless and desperate, parents end up going back to the drawing board. "Fixing" your child's behavior does not work. Why? Because behavior is not the problem.

Learning the Hard Way

Over the past dozen years, I have worked with hundreds of families and children of all ages as a family relationship coach, adult educator, teacher, nanny, babysitter, and tutor. Based on my research, experience, and best practices, I have developed the empirically-proven Parenting Connection Approach to creating parent-child relationships built on mutual, unconditional love, trust, and deep connection.

Although I now confidently share my knowledge with parents and educators, I haven't always known the answers.

When I graduated from university with a master's degree in education, I believed—somewhat naively—that I knew everything I needed to help my students become smart, happy, and successful in life. I was certain that teaching was going to be fun and easy. I thought I would teach, and students would just sit and listen. I was sure that just because you were an adult, especially if you are a parent or teacher, children's respect came automatically.

When I found myself in classrooms of over thirty out-of-control students who could care less about what I had to say, let alone learn from me, I quickly realized I was wrong. I would explain to myself that I was unlucky to get the students who weren't well-behaved. I just needed to teach them how to behave.

Wanting what was best for my students, I believed that "fixing" my students' behavior was the solution. I became strict and demanding. I would tell them what to do and how, hold them accountable, and proudly reward and praise them when they listened. I also wouldn't hesitate to lecture, shame, or scold them when they didn't.

That approach did not work well. The stricter and more demanding I became, the more resistance I encountered, the more challenging it was for me to build relationships with them, and the more frustrated and upset my students and I became with each other. The students would ignore and argue with me, roll their eyes at me, make fun of me, or simply refuse to follow my directions.

I would often end up in what I thought were "power struggles," which I'd sworn to avoid. Those "power struggles" left me feeling frustrated, disappointed, and helpless. I was not proud of the way I handled myself in those situations and often regretted my actions.

It took me a while to accept reality and finally realize that *I* was the one who needed to learn more, and *my* behavior and *my* approach were what needed to change.

Worn out by constant fighting and feeling guilty for treating my students too strictly, the only solution I saw at that time was to turn around and head in the opposite direction. I believed that if I made my students happy by being incredibly friendly, they would like me, listen, and be nicer to me. I became that kind, patient, and understanding teacher that I thought every student wanted to have. I tolerated their inappropriate behavior, outbursts, and hurtful words. I hid my true feelings because I didn't want them to feel guilty and pretended like I was fine when I felt hurt, disrespected, or wanted to cry.

When I did not feel treated well, I found excuses for them —I would remind myself that they were having a hard day, had family issues, didn't get enough sleep or food, or whatever it might be that was upsetting them—and kept accepting the poor treatment I received.

I thought that being nice, compassionate, and kind, no matter what, was the key to building mutually respectful and trusting relationships. The nicer you are, the more respected and appreciated you will be. I wanted my students to realize that I didn't enjoy fighting them; my only intent was to help. I was at a loss for words when my students began behaving in even more disrespectful and arrogant ways in response to my new approach.

I felt that what I was doing for them was being taken for granted. Even worse, it seemed like I was expected to tolerate everything they would throw at me. I kept telling myself that their disrespectful way of treating me would not last for long. I believed they would eventually appreciate how nice and patient I was and would begin treating me the way I was treating them. I waited and waited, but that appreciation and respect just never came.

The longer I patiently tolerated my students' poor attitudes, the worse their behavior and attitudes became. They became *more* demanding, unsatisfied, and disagreeable. The more I tried to please them, the harder it became to do so. Once again, I had to admit that what I was doing was not working. So, what was the answer?

On my quest to find out what I could do to get my students to behave, I read dozens of books on classroom management, completed numerous local training courses on managing children's behavior, and asked for advice from more experienced teachers. I learned many effective management strategies and techniques. As I changed my approach by improving my behavior management skills, the students changed as well. Before I knew it, the very same children who once treated me horribly began to listen to me. I felt like I had found a win-win strategy.

At last, I had compliant learners who followed my instructions without talking back, putting me down, or rolling their eyes at me. This change in behavior felt like a great accomplishment! However, I quickly noticed something that troubled me. Even though they became polite and compliant, they seemed distant. They would not approach me with questions, share their opinions, or engage in conversation. It became clear to me that they were simply performing what I asked them to do so they would not get in trouble and just be left alone. Everything felt too rigid, robot-like, emotionless. I felt like my students were not being themselves when around me but rather pretending to be who I expected them to be.

Only once I got students to listen to me did I realize that getting children to listen and behave was not the answer. It became evident to me there was something I was missing. I succeeded in developing excellent management skills, but I failed in developing what mattered most: connection in my relationships with students. I wanted my students to be open and authentic with me. I wanted them to feel comfortable being themselves, asking for help, and sharing their true feelings and challenges with me so that I could support and encourage them. That became my new mission.

The Missing Piece

As an English Language Learner Specialist at an elementary school, I taught multiple grade levels and classes as well as co-taught with different classroom teachers. I saw how dozens of teachers taught and interacted with their students. I began watching them with extraordinary curiosity, a ferocious thirst for learning, and sincere gratitude for the opportunity to observe and learn from the teachers' and their students' experiences. I would not only observe colleagues at the schools where I worked, but I would ask educators from other schools, my colleagues' friends' friends, and teachers I hardly knew if I could come to observe them. The effectiveness and level of their skills didn't matter to me. I wanted to see it all because I wanted to learn both what to do and what not to do.

I attended trainings on teacher-student relationship building and communication and used every opportunity, even the shortest break, to relentlessly ask presenters questions at every training I attended. With time, I discovered some common themes, patterns, and insights, and my understanding of human nature and relationships deepened.

By applying my knowledge and skills as I learned them, I

gradually created connected teacher-student relationships and helped my students form meaningful relationships with each other. We became more than just students and teacher. We became a family. We looked forward to class. We laughed and had fun learning. We enjoyed openly and honestly sharing our opinions and knowledge. We supported and encouraged each other.

Everything seemed to be going well. I felt that I had finally built the teacher-student relationships I wanted and developed the skills I needed to prepare my students for the real world. I was successfully equipping them with solid academic knowledge, belief in themselves, and strong relationship skills.

Yet, there was still something I was not at peace with. Every time I saw students sitting in the hallway after being sent from their classroom for defiance, and sometimes even violence, I felt like there was something we, as a society, were missing. I spent many sleepless nights thinking about those "behavior" students who society is always trying to "fix." As usual, I turned to books and trainings to look for the missing piece, but I ended up finding it in the place I least expected. The answer was sitting there in the hallway with the "behavior" students.

One day, I was walking down the hallway to my next class, preoccupied with reviewing in my mind the lesson plans I was going to teach. *Wham!* A classroom door burst open, and I looked up to see a fourth-grade boy storming out of the classroom toward the chairs where the unruly students were sent. Not noticing me, he flopped into the chair as if someone had physically hurled him onto it. It seemed like his body could not hold that immense, built-up rage any longer, and he let it all out through his body language now that he was sure nobody could see him.

Knowing his violent reputation, I knew that I was taking a risk when I approached him, but, seeing how upset he was, I simply could not pass him by. I grabbed a nearby chair and moved it next to him so that we could talk.

"What happened?" I asked the upset boy. I had taught in his class before, so we knew each other a little.

Getting all tense and angry again, he went on and on blaming his teacher and other students for everything that happened. When he was done venting his range, he suddenly got quiet as if he just realized something. Then, he put his face in his hands and half-whispered, "I'm embarrassed..."

My heart broke for this boy. I could feel his pain. I remembered similar moments in my life when I had acted less than my best, had a hard time dealing with my emotions, and felt guilty for saying hurtful things I didn't really mean to the people I loved. Back then, I wanted to change, but I had no idea how. Just like I used to, this child felt as if something was wrong with him because he could not handle his emotions and actions in a non-violent, emotionally healthy way.

The truth was there was nothing wrong with him. He simply did not have the skills he needed yet. He did not know how to connect with himself by becoming aware of, accepting, and honoring his feelings and thoughts while being compassionate, loving, and kind toward himself. At that moment, I realized what we, as a society, were missing— teaching children how to connect with themselves. I also sadly realized that I was not equipped to do so, but my desire to help was so strong that I felt confident I would learn how to help.

I decided to research by digging deeper into the issue. I studied neuroscience, neuro-linguistic programming, and human psychology to understand brain functions and human behavior better. I deepened my knowledge of linguistics and sociology to improve my own and my students' communication skills. I learned more about emotional intelligence and mindset from experts in their fields and some of the world's most renown thinkers, psychologists, and leaders, such as Nelson Mandela, Napoleon Hill, Anthony Robbins, Richard Bandler, Virginia Satir, Mahatma Gandhi, Mark Goulston, Stephen Covey, and Eckhart Tolle. I sought as much knowledge as I could through reading books, but also by attending online webinars, courses, and in-person seminars and trainings.

My research required a lot of time, trial and error, financial investment, and effort. Most importantly, it required me to question all my beliefs to identify the common misconceptions that I had acquired while learning to connect with myself on a deeper level than ever before.

All this resulted in designing my own approach based on the most profound concepts I had learned from others and my own experiences. I was finally able to help students connect with themselves by learning how to allow, embrace, and process their emotions. As a result, their relationships with me, other teachers, other students, and parents improved. Most importantly, their relationship with themselves improved. They became happier and more comfortable being who they were as well as more conscientious, caring, and compassionate toward others.

Over time, other teachers began noticing the changes and asked me how I was able to get such inspiring results. So, I started sharing my approach with them. Teachers were amazed at how well it worked for them in their classrooms!

I thought, *If this approach works for teachers, it could be so much more impactful if parents also applied it.* Parents have the most significant impact on their children. I know they can achieve even greater transformational success in their parent-child relationships by applying an approach that already works well in classrooms. Regardless of how important other adults in your child's life are, *your* opinion, love, and approval mean the most to your child, even when he shows and acts as if they don't. Your child cares about you and what you have to say.

When parents incorporated what they learned from me,

they discovered remarkable transformations in their children's behaviors. By learning to understand and connect with themselves and their children, parents have been able to truly experience the joy and fulfillment unique to a parent-child relationship.

Change Is Possible

If you and your child are not feeling fully connected for any reason, and your relationship does not bring you or your child the joy and fulfillment you were hoping for, don't beat yourself up. Ask yourself, "Is this the parent-child relationship I have always dreamt of?" If your answer is "no," stop ignoring your frustrations and concerns. Listen to your heart and decide whether this is how you want you and your child to live your lives. Settle for the relationship you have or transform it into the relationship that you both deserve.

The truth is that if you are not happy with your relationship with your child right now and are simply hoping that it will change with time, you are right—it will. But most likely not in the way you are hoping for. A relationship is alive and dynamic, and it either evolves or deteriorates. If your relationship has been deteriorating, it is a sign that the approach you've been using does not work. For your relationship to evolve, improve, and grow, you need to use a better approach.

While you may feel hesitant about whether you can change anything in your relationship, I want to assure you that the approach I am going to teach you has proven that change is possible for anyone who commits to taking action.

If you want to have the parent-child relationship you have always dreamed of, stop focusing on how to get your child to behave, and begin focusing on learning to connect with yourself and your child.

When you and your child are emotionally connected:

- You feel more peaceful, joyful, and empowered.
- You trust and are open with one another.
- You feel accepted, appreciated, and comfortable being yourselves.

When you feel emotionally connected, it will also be easier for you to set boundaries, feel and be understood, and share your knowledge and wisdom with your child.

As we are about to embark on our journey together, before you turn to the next page, make sure to bring along self-love, patience, and open-mindedness. This will be an insightful, worthwhile, life-changing journey for you and your child. May this book become your guide, inspiration, and a reminder to believe in yourself and your child!

PART I

THE FOUNDATION FOR A FULLY CONNECTED PARENT-CHILD RELATIONSHIP

1

WHY WE ACT THE WAY WE ACT

Although challenging behavior may often seem irrational and confusing, the truth is that there is a reason why we act the way we do. When you understand how the human brain works, you will understand and be able to connect with yourself and your child better.

Understanding the Human Brain

"No! I'm not wearing that red dress!" yelled Lizzy, throwing her dress across her bedroom as hard as she could. Clenching her fists along her body and stomping her feet, with her face all red, Lizzy was making her point: there was no way she was going to listen to her mother and wear the dress that she picked out for her.

Lizzy wanted to wear her favorite black-and-white dress. Her mother, Rosalind, tried to explain to Lizzy why she needed to wear the red dress, but Lizzy kept yelling, "No! No! I'm not wearing that red dress, and you can't make me!"

It was the morning of Rainbow Day at Lizzy's school. Each grade level was supposed to wear an assigned rainbow color. Lizzy's Kindergarten class was assigned red. It was already past 7:30 a.m., yet Lizzy was still in her pajamas. Rosalind knew they were going to be late for school if they did not leave the house right away, but she had no idea what to do.

"When she's like that," explained Rosalind, "I feel like she doesn't even hear me." And she was certainly right!

That is exactly what happens when we are in stressful and overwhelming situations. Even though Lizzy technically heard Rosalind's voice, Rosalind's explanations and reasoning did not make sense or matter to Lizzy.

Rosalind had enough and yelled back at her daughter. She told Lizzy that she would be in trouble if she did not put the red dress on right away. This experience clearly weakened the connection between the mother and daughter, but what is less apparent is how it was the result of how the brain works under stress.

What You Need to Know about the Brain

You can better understand why you and your child react so intensely in stressful situations by becoming familiar with how the brain works. When explaining the brain's structure and function to families I work with, for simplicity's sake, I use the well-known, three-brain model, initially proposed by American physician and neuroscientist Paul MacLean in his triune brain theory in the 1960s.[1]

According to this model, the human brain is composed of three vertical parts—the primal brain (also referred to as the reptilian brain because it resembles the entire brain of a reptile) at the bottom, the emotional brain (the midbrain, which is often called the limbic system), and the thinking brain (the cerebral cortex) at the top. While functioning together as a whole, each of the brains has its own responsibility and greatly influences our behavior.

1. **The primal brain** supports essential life functions, such as breathing, heart rate, and sleep, which ensure our survival. Because it focuses on our survival, it is also in charge of the three F's, which we will discuss later in this chapter.
2. **The emotional brain** is responsible for memories and generating emotions.
3. **The thinking brain** is in charge of higher thinking, reasoning, planning, impulse control, decision making, and emotion management.

Amygdala Hijack

The amygdala is a set of neurons located in the emotional brain that play a crucial role in protecting us by detecting potential danger and causing us to feel fear in order to take action. Fear is a survival mechanism that functions as a warning sign. Most of the time, the amygdala allows the thinking brain to take over and make a decision about how to respond to the situation. When under stress, however, the amygdala generates fear and puts the primal brain in charge.

This phenomenon was named *the amygdala hijack* by psychologist Daniel Goleman, the author of *Emotional Intelligence: Why It Can Matter More Than IQ*.[2] In response to fear, the primal brain automatically initiates what is known as the Fight, Flight, Freeze, or F3, response, which was first described by American neurologist and physiologist Walter Bradford Cannon as a "flight or fight" response.[3]

The F3 Response

Does the Fight, Flight, Freeze response serve us? Absolutely! It ensures our safety and survival by causing us to take immediate action. When attacked by a wild animal, a person would increase their chance of survival by fighting the animal (fight response), running away (flight response), or staying still, hoping the predator loses interest and wanders off (freeze response). The problem is that when the amygdala is "hijacked," the primal brain causes us to react the same way to *perceived* danger as we would to *real* danger.

If you do not train your thinking brain to intervene before the amygdala hijack occurs, the amygdala will cause your primal brain to apply one of the F3 responses in both cases—when you see your child about to get hit by a car (real danger) and when your child is screaming at you (perceived danger). While taking one of the F3 responses can be justified and vital in the former case, it can only damage your relationship with your child in the latter.

The F3 Response in Action

By understanding how the brain works, we can now explain Lizzy's behavior and her mother's reaction. We will focus on Lizzy first.

Although Lizzy's behavior may seem disrespectful, unloving, and selfish, the true underlying reason for her behavior is that her caring primal brain was trying to protect her from the perceived danger—not getting her needs met, which, for the brain, is equal to not surviving.

"Now, what on Earth does not being allowed to wear her favorite dress have to do with Lizzy's survival?" you may ask. "Why does Lizzy perceive that as a danger? It does not make sense." It seems illogical and unreasonable at first.

That was what used to perplex me when I encountered such behavior in my students. I felt confused and incompetent until I found the American author, psychotherapist, and "mother of family therapy," Virginia Satir's explanation about "fear of the unknown." "Most people think the will to survive is the strongest instinct in human beings, but it isn't. The strongest instinct is to keep things familiar."[4] She explains that

6

"when we change anything that's been ongoing, we have the strong temptation to go with what's familiar."[5]

Understanding and knowing what, when, and how something will happen, and how to handle it gives us a sense of safety. We then feel prepared, calm, and ready. On the other hand, when we do not understand or know what will happen, how to handle it, or what to do if the plan fails, we feel scared. That is why we perceive change as dangerous. We get comfortable and feel safe in familiar situations. As soon as something unexpected or new happens, we become fearful. That is exactly what happened to Lizzy.

In her mind, she decided that she was going to wear the black-and-white dress. She had certainty about what was going to happen. She had a plan. When her mother told her that she had to wear a specific color, Lizzy's certainty was suddenly shaken by the unexpected change. Her primal brain went into survival mode, which caused Lizzy to use fight response to overcome the perceived danger that she was not prepared for.

Becoming Aware of Your Emotional State

We will now return to Rosalind to understand why she ended up yelling at Lizzy despite her attempt to connect with her daughter.

Because of the way Lizzy acted—yelling and refusing to do what Rosalind asked her to do, Rosalind felt unloved and disrespected by her daughter. Rosalind was afraid that if she did not do something to stop her daughter's "disrespectful" behavior, Lizzy's behavior would escalate, or she would learn that it was acceptable to treat her mother that way. So, Rosalind threatened her daughter that she would be in trouble.

Just like Rosalind, when a child acts the way Lizzy did in a stressful situation, many parents often interpret such behavior as unloving and disrespectful. "I can't believe she does this to me. She must not love me," parents conclude. They are afraid that they are raising an uncompassionate, disrespectful child. Parents may feel like they are failing as parents in their child's or society's eyes. "How did I allow us to even get here? I'm not a good parent if my daughter behaves this way. I failed to teach her how to behave well."

Many parents are afraid that if they do not teach their child the appropriate behavior right when the child displays it, it will be too late to teach it to her later. They believe that their child will continue to behave in a socially unacceptable manner, which will affect her social and personal life. They are justifiably worried that their child will not be able to have positive relationships with her friends and family, which will likely increase the child's stress and decrease the child's quality of life. Therefore, the most common parental reaction in such situations is to focus on changing the child's behavior immediately.

Parents are also afraid of disconnecting with their children by losing their love. This has a lot to do with their needs (which we will discuss in the following chapters) and the primal brain function. Subconsciously, they equate what they see as the child's unloving and disrespectful behavior with their own survival. They understandably fear that if the child learns to disrespect them, the child will feel disconnected from them and might not be willing to be part of the parents' lives in the future. Parents worry that when they get older or when something happens to them, they will not be able to count on their child's care and support.

Therefore, stressful situations like this evoke fear in parents and are hard not to take personally. If the feeling is not dealt with appropriately, it may cause the parents to go into one of the F3 responses. As a result, a parent may yell back at the child, as in the case with Rosalind (fight response), give in to whatever the child demands to avoid conflict, if Rosalind said,

"Ok, ok, you can take the black-and-white dress. Just don't get upset," (flight response), or just stand there having no idea what to do and hope that the problem will somehow eventually go away (freeze response). No matter which of the F3 responses a parent chooses, the response may cause the connection between the parent and child to weaken.

When parents are under stress, they often attempt to connect with their children without noticing that they themselves are not ready. Parents need to check in with themselves to make sure that they are in a self-connected state. They need to ensure that they are not acting out of unconscious fear created by their primal brain but from a conscious, loving, and calm place.

If Rosalind had taken a moment to connect with herself first and tame her primal brain by putting her thinking brain in charge, she would have been able to choose an action that would help her connect with her daughter.

That is why parents need to connect with themselves first in order to avoid becoming victims of their primal brain's reaction to fear. Parents need to remember the following four truths about the primal brain to stay connected with themselves and their child. These truths are pertinent to both your brain and your child's brain.

The Three Truths about the Primal Brain

1. The primal brain looks for easy ways to meet your needs. Why does an exhausted mother give in to her son's whim to have a cupcake before going to bed, even though the mother knows that it's not good for him, and the family's rule is no desserts before bedtime? Why does a tired father put his toddler daughter's shoes on for her when she refuses to do so, even though he knows that she can put her shoes on by herself? Because it saves energy. It's easier to give in than to reteach, convince, or possibly have to deal with a tantrum or an argument.

Designed to ensure your survival, one of the primal brain's goals is to save you energy by looking for easy ways to meet your needs. The problem is that what's easy is not always what's best for you and your child. Learn to make choices in your and your child's best interests, even though it may mean you have to choose what's hard.

2. The primal brain seeks instant gratification. Remember how impatient children get when they want something? The primal brain has a hard time waiting. It wants what it wants, and it wants it right now! The urge can be so strong that a child may feel that if he doesn't get what he wants right away, he'll die!

The same is true for the parent's brain. Parents want to get the desired results as soon as possible. Why do you think many parents keep buying gifts for their children, even though they have promised themselves to save money? It's because buying gifts and seeing how their children react to them with surprise and excitement feels good.

Prioritizing the primal brain's urge for instant gratification often results in a poor parent-child relationship and raising a child who takes things for granted, struggles with patience and resilience, and does not know how to practice delayed gratification.

3. The primal brain protects you from pain. Interpreting pain, both physical and emotional, as a threat to your survival, the primal brain wants to help you avoid it. This primal brain's life-saving function is vital in many cases, but not when that pain is harmless and necessary for you or your child to grow. It may feel painful to keep your word and not to take your child to camp because she has chosen to dishonor your boundaries. However, if you decide to go through that temporary emotional discomfort, you will feel good about yourself for having integrity by honoring your personal boundaries and will teach your child to honor them. By going through emotional discomfort, you will also develop a trusting and respectful parent-child relationship.

Learning to distinguish between life-threatening physical and emotional pain and temporary discomfort will lead to a stronger parent-child relationship.

Mirror Neurons

I remember lying on the bed wearing glasses and reading a newspaper when I heard my mom's voice whispering to someone, "Come here. Look!" I turned my head and saw my mother standing with a relative, pointing at me and laughing. What? I was just reading. There was nothing funny about it! Except that I had just turned four years old, was laying on my relative's bed with one foot over the other (his favorite position), wearing his glasses, and reading his newspaper, which was not only upside down but written in a foreign language. At that age, I didn't even know how to read in my own language! What was I doing, exactly? I was imitating my relative without giving it any thought.

I bet you have noticed your child doing the same. It might be your son reaching out for his toy phone when he sees you talking on the phone or your daughter repeating your encouragement, "You've got it, sweetheart. I believe in you!" when playing with her dolls. How can we explain that? Their mirror neurons are at work.

Mirror neurons activate when we perform an action or observe another performing the same action. This phenomenon was discovered in the 1990s by a group of Italian neuroscientists, directed by Giacomo Rizzolatti from the University of Parma, studying the brain of a monkey.[6] The neuroscientists noticed that the same group of neurons fired in the monkey's brain when the monkey saw a researcher pick up a peanut and eat it that had fired when the monkey had eaten a peanut. They also realized mirror neurons would fire only when the action was intentional.[7] Mirror neurons do not respond to random, meaningless hand movements, but if we use our hand for a specific purpose— pick up a spoon to eat some oatmeal or press a remote-control button to play music—they will activate. Mirror neurons help the child learn, often subconsciously, by imitating another's behavior.

Have you noticed your child not paying attention to the toy truck lying on the floor next to him until his little sister picks it up and begins playing with it? Suddenly, it sparks your son's interest, and he wants to have that truck right away. If you don't know about mirror neurons, you may assume that the child is just being selfish and may get frustrated with or even punish the child when he decides to take the toy from his sister. That is why it is important to understand that such behavior is often the result of the effect mirror neurons have on us. So, the common saying "Monkey see, monkey do" was not only confirmed by the Italian group of scientists but proved to be true about people as well.

Emotional Contagion

There is another effect mirror neurons have on us. Have you ever come home in a good mood to a cranky child? What happens to your good mood? It quickly disappears. What about having a bad day at work and looking at a photo of your child grinning from ear to ear? Automatically, a smile appears on your face.

This is the effect of mirror neurons in action. This phenomenon is called *emotional contagion*, which is "a process through which a person or group influence the emotions and emotional behavior of another person or group."[8] Just as you pick up your child's emotions, your child picks up and imitates yours.

Why is it essential for you to know about emotional contagion and how it relates to your parent-child relationship? As you learned in the part on the primal brain, when unpleasant emotions run high, we can perceive others as threats. We don't want to connect with someone we see as a threat. In order to connect with another, we need to feel safe around that person, trust them, and be willing to be vulnerable with them. That is why both you and your child need to be in a calm, safe place emotionally to connect.

When your child is angry, stressed, or anxious, you can create a calm and safe place by connecting with yourself first and establishing a peaceful state within yourself. The child's mirror neurons will eventually "mirror" your state. You feeling peaceful and calm will help your child arrive at the same place. When you meet in a shared, peaceful place, you have the opportunity to connect.

Connect through Understanding

The physicist and chemist Marie Curie said, "Nothing in life is to be feared. It is only to be understood." Understanding how your brain and your child's brain operate and affect your behavior will help you eliminate your fear of the unknown and avoid falling into the F3 mode. It will also help you not take things personally and remain compassionate and confident in stressful situations. Understanding why you and your child behave the way each of you does will help you stay out of your child's emotional swirl and help her get out of it while remaining self-connected.

When you are self-connected, you feel calm, think more clearly, and avoid overreaction. You are also more likely to remember and apply the principles and concepts that you will be learning in this book more effectively to connect with your child when you are self-connected. When your child feels connected to you, she will be more open to listening to what you are teaching her and will make an effort to understand your perspective.

Practicing connecting with yourself first, processing your emotions, and evoking the emotions that will serve you and your child is key to a fully connected parent-child relationship. You will learn more about all of this in the following chapters.

But what about your child? Would it be fair to count on her to be able to do the same? To a large extent, it depends on your understanding of how your child's brain is different from yours and the support and guidance you give your child to promote her brain's healthy development.

Why We Act the Way We Act
Action Step

Take the first step toward creating a connected parent-child relationship by going to your *Parenting Connection Workbook* and completing the exercises about the F3 responses you and your child use. This workbook is my gift to you. You can download it at www.albinspire.com/workbook.

2

HOW YOUR CHILD'S BRAIN WORKS

"Stand up right now and go back into the classroom, or I will have to call your parents. You can't just leave class whenever you want." Ignoring the principal's ultimatum, first-grader Emin kept inconsolably crying while lying down on the hallway floor. As a teacher's aide was walking by, she couldn't help but stop and ask the assistant principal for permission to talk to the boy. Desperate after failing to find a way to get the boy back to class, the principal nodded.

The teacher's aide crouched down next to the boy, gently placed her hand on his knee, and in a soft, quiet voice said, "I know it can be overwhelming in class when you don't understand much of what is being taught. It happens. But running away and lying here on the floor is neither safe nor going to solve the problem. I would like to take you back to class. Just hold my hand when you are ready." She stretched her hand out to Emin while remaining in a crouched position. Emin gulped down a sob, took the teacher's aide's hand, and followed her back to the classroom.

The two adults who tried to help Emin ended up having very different results. Why? Because the teacher's aide knew something about how a child's brain works that the principal didn't. She knew that giving a child an ultimatum would not work because a child's brain does not work the same way as an adult's.

The Challenge of the Child's Brain

Wouldn't it be great if your child could always be happy and well-behaved? Don't you wish he would regulate his emotions and always make rational decisions based on logic? What about reading your emotions to know when you are not in the mood for his requests? "Hey, Mom and Dad, you're clearly tired after a long day. I had a challenging day myself, but I was able to handle it just fine. I'll be up in my room, finishing my homework. Let me know if you need anything."

Yes, that would be wonderful! Although it may not seem possible to you right now, this could be your reality. Once you learn to understand your child's brain and apply that knowledge to your parenting, you will be able to teach your child to use his brain to deal with any emotion so that he can make emotionally intelligent decisions in a way that helps him and others in his life.

The challenge is that we, as adults, often have a hard time ourselves dealing with our emotions in stressful situations. That is despite our thinking brain being developed enough for us to be in charge of our emotional brain in order to handle our emotions well.

For a child, his challenge is even greater when it comes to dealing with his emotions. Research shows that the frontal cortex (frontal lobe)—the rational part of a child's brain—matures more slowly than other structures of the brain and is not fully developed until the mid-twenties.[1] This part of the brain is responsible for executive functions such as "planning appropriate behavioral responses to external and internal stimuli,"[2] judgment, decision-making, and attention span of your child. How this relates to your child is that he is more likely to live in the moment, act on impulse, and think irrationally. For example, your child might run across the street to catch the butterfly he saw on the other side without first checking if the road is clear.

Two Approaches to Avoid

You might be thinking, "Does that mean I have to wait until my child's brain is fully developed in his mid-twenties for him to act responsibly and make more rational choices?" That is the conclusion some parents mistakenly make after learning about the child's brain development. By thinking that there is not much that can be done except wait for the child to be ready for more mature conversations, responsibilities, and self-reliance, parents usually take one of two approaches.

Some parents, wanting to be helpful and understanding, lovingly tolerate any kind of behavior and do things that the child refuses to do for himself, believing that he is too young to behave more responsibly and independently. The parents who take this approach unintentionally use their knowledge of the child's brain development as an excuse for his behavior.

How often have you heard parents explain their child's behavior by saying, "Oh, she is just too young to understand," when their five-year-old refuses to listen to them? How about a parent allowing his three-year-old son to clumsily hold his expensive phone while he watches a video? "He is going through his toddler 'no' stage right now. He wants to do everything by himself and gets very upset when I try to help him." This approach often leads to enabling the child. He ends up blaming his parents and others for his misfortune. He has difficulties regulating his emotions, bursts of aggression, egocentric tendencies, low self-worth, and poor personal and professional relationships.

The approach other parents choose is to attempt to

control situations and their child's behavior by making all of the decisions for the child, often without explaining the reason behind their decisions. Parents who take this approach are convinced that explaining their reasoning wouldn't make sense because the child would not understand anyway. This approach may often lead to authoritarian-style parenting.

How often do you hear parents tell their child, "You should never say that!" or "You never do it right! Next time, ask me before doing anything." How about when their child asks why, they respond, "Because I said so," believing that the child is either saying that simply to challenge them or feeling irritated by the request because they are certain that giving a detailed explanation would be just a waste of time since the child would not understand it anyway? This approach often causes the child to eventually rebel against his parents' rules and beliefs and creates tension, emotional suffering, or hostility in a parent-child relationship. It often results in the child's constant self-doubt, inability to make decisions independently, difficulty regulating his emotions, aggressive behavior outside, and, in some cases, inside, the home, as well as resentment and blame toward his parents when he grows up.

As you can see, neither of these approaches is healthy for a parent-child relationship. If waiting until your child's brain is fully developed in his mid-twenties while doing everything for him or making all the decisions for him isn't the answer, then what *is*?

Changing Your Child's Brain

You can help your child make rational and responsible choices by teaching your child to use the power of his brain to biologically change itself through *brain integration*—strengthening connections between the parts of his brain—

and *neuroplasticity*—formation of new connections between the neurons (nerve cells) in his brain.

Brain Integration

The human brain has many parts. You are already familiar with the three of them located vertically—the primal brain, the emotional brain, and the thinking brain.

There are also two parts of the brain, the connection between which influences your child's behavior choices as well as emotional, mental, and physical well-being. In his "Split-Brain Experiments," conducted with his colleagues, neurobiologist Roger W. Sperry found that the thinking brain is divided into two hemispheres located horizontally and symmetrically to each other—the left hemisphere and the right hemisphere.[3]

His theory argues that each of the brain's hemispheres has its own function. The left hemisphere is responsible for logic, language, planning, rational thinking, and order. It is more directly connected and influenced by the thinking brain. The right hemisphere is responsible for emotions, non-verbal cues, creativity, and intuition. This hemisphere is more directly connected and influenced by the emotional brain.

Daniel Siegel and Tina Payne Bryson call the process of strengthening the connection between the parts of the brain *integration*. They explain that integration "coordinates and balances the separate regions of the brain that link together." Dr. Siegel and Dr. Bryson point out that for children to use their whole brain in a coordinated way, we need to support their brain's *horizontal integration*, "so that their left-brain logic can work well with their right-brain emotion," and *vertical integration*, "so that the physically higher parts of their brain, which let them thoughtfully consider their actions, work well with the lower parts, which are more concerned with instinct, gut reaction, and survival."[4]

Helping your child integrate the brain vertically and horizontally will increase his *emotional intelligence.* Dan Goleman popularized the concept of emotional intelligence (E.I.) in his 1995 book *Emotional Intelligence.*[5] "Emotional intelligence is your ability to recognize and understand emotions in yourself and others, and your ability to use this awareness to manage your behavior and relationships."[6] The development of E.I. is necessary for the child to connect with himself and others.

Neuroplasticity

When I told Jennifer that her eight-year-old son Travis could learn to behave differently, she was skeptical. "Maybe this brain stuff works for other children, but I don't think it's going to work for Travis. He's always been this way. He's just like his father—stubborn and uncooperative. You can't fight against genes. Besides, he has picked up all these bad habits from his friends. His behavior is already wired in him."

While Jennifer had a point—some brain pre-wiring is indeed influenced by genetic inheritance and habits—what she didn't know was that the desired behavior change was still possible. Researchers have discovered that the human brain is not as hard-wired as previously believed. In the early 1900s, it was discovered that neurons in the brain could "reorganize" themselves by forming new neural connections throughout life. This ability of the brain to change is called neuroplasticity. A Canadian neuropsychologist Donald Hebb explained it as "neurons that fire together, wire together,"[7] which is often referred to as Hebb's Law.

Neural pathways are formed based on our thoughts, experiences, and behaviors. These neural pathways get reinforced through repetition. We become good at what we practice regularly. When we keep practicing a thought or behavior, at some point, it becomes habitual and subconscious. It begins to reside in our primal brain. That's our brain's way of making our lives easier by saving us energy and allowing us to be efficient.

It is how you can explain reading an email or a text message without consciously thinking about every reading rule you learned in Kindergarten. Your brain does not go, "When two vowels go walking, the first one does the talking," when you see the word "read." You probably don't even remember the rule itself because you don't need it anymore. Your brain does all the "decoding" in reading on autopilot.

Children's brains work in precisely the same way. By repeating certain behaviors, they make those behaviors habitual. That is the basis of learning. It works well if they practice the behaviors that serve them, but what if they don't?

The fact is the brain does not recognize the difference between helpful and harmful habits and applies the same process, which means that the brain can make both helpful and harmful behaviors part of the child's subconscious mind. The more often a behavior is repeated and reinforced, the stronger the neural pathways will be. Once neurons form strong neural pathways, it requires some time and deliberate practice to rewire neurons for the child to behave differently.

The good news is that, through neuroplasticity, you can help your child learn new behaviors and unlearn old behaviors. Additionally, the plasticity of the brain is even more phenomenal in children than adults. Due to their brain developing rapidly and new neural connections being formed every day at a greater frequency and speed than in an adult brain, acquiring a new skill, developing a new habit, or learning a new behavior is much easier in childhood than in adulthood.[8] This is why childhood, especially early childhood (usually defined as birth to eight years old), is the best time to teach your child.

The more integrated the regions of the brain are and the stronger the connections between the neurons are, the more capable the child is of connecting with himself and others in order to deal with his emotions in a healthy and productive way and consciously create the life he wants.

Actively Creating the Relationship You Deserve

When you understand how the human brain works and how your child's brain is different from yours, you are able to understand yourself, your child, and your behaviors on a much deeper level. This profound understanding will enable you to actively make changes by consciously choosing and teaching your child to choose behaviors that serve him and bring you closer together instead of passively observing what is happening in your parent-child relationship, feeling helpless, and waiting for things to become better. Learning about your child's needs and how to help him meet them in constructive ways in the next chapter will help you even more in developing a strong emotional connection.

How Your Child's Brain Works
Action Step

Take a moment to go to your *Parenting Connection Workbook* to answer specific questions to help you deepen your understanding of how your child's brain impacts his behavior.

3

YOUR CHILD'S NEEDS

"Just be aware that he is one of those negative attention seekers who doesn't respect adult authority," I was warned before I began to work with one of my new first-graders, Elijah.

When I entered the classroom, the teacher was heading to the carpet area. I used this moment to come up to Elijah, who was sitting on a beanbag in the back of the room, and introduce myself. "Hello, Elijah! Welcome to our school. My name is Ms. Terpetska," I offered my hand for a handshake. Elijah looked at me, then at my hand, and turned away.

The teacher asked everyone to join her on the carpet, but Elijah didn't move. Deciding to give Elijah space, I went on to support other students I worked with in the class. After the lesson was over, I let Elijah know that I was there to support him and other students with reading in a small group. In a raised voice, he harshly responded, "I don't want to! I don't like you all!" A common reaction might be to tell him how rude and disrespectful he was toward other students and me. However, my knowledge of the six human needs allowed me to take a different approach.

"I hear you, Elijah. You don't feel like joining the group

for reading right now. You can read alone if that's what you need. Feel free to join us when you are ready," I said casually and walked away.

As the group of students and I were reading a book, I could see from the corner of my eye that Elijah was watching us. Then, he took off his shoe and calculatedly threw it in our direction.

I stopped reading for a second and looked up at Elijah. "You are always welcome to join us when you feel like it, Elijah," and continued reading to the students.

Elijah sat there for a while. Then, he got up to get his shoe. He stood still and looked at us while holding his shoe in his hand and eventually asked, "Can we read my book?"

A moment later, we were lively reading Elijah's book as a group. Along with other students, Elijah was giggling and having fun using different voices for different characters.

Had this happened at the beginning of my teaching career, before I learned about the six human needs, my response to the situation would have been very different. Considering the way he talked to me and threw his shoe in class, I would have been thinking of what consequence to give him for such disrespectful behavior. "Knowing" that he was doing it "on purpose" just to "to get me," I would have taken it personally and would not have missed a chance to make it clear to the new student who was in charge there. That type of interaction would have hurt our student-teacher relationship from the very beginning. Instead, my knowledge of the six human needs helped me not take Elijah's attitude personally, understand what needs were driving Elijah's behavior, and help him meet them in a constructive way.

So, what are those needs? Why do you need to know them? And how can you use your knowledge of human needs to build a strong connection with your child?

According to a world-renowned innovator and teacher of family and strategic therapy Cloé Madanes, "all of us have basic needs, not merely desires but profound needs that underlie and motivate every choice we make."[1] These needs are:

Certainty/Comfort/Security: We want to feel safe, protected, and comfortable. We want to avoid physical and emotional pain. We want order, predictability, and consistency in our lives.

Uncertainty/Variety: At times, our bodies and minds get tired and bored from predictability, repetition, and routine. When we feel bored, we want some variety in our lives.

Significance: Every single one of us wants to feel significant. We all want to feel that we matter, our voice is heard, and our presence is acknowledged. We want to feel special and unique.

Love/Connection: We all need a sense of belonging and connection with other human beings, especially our caregivers. We also crave love from the moment that we are born.

Growth: Everyone has the need to grow. We have only two ways to go—either progress and develop physically, emotionally, intellectually, and spiritually—or regress.

Contribution: An inherent part of human nature is contributing, helping, and supporting others, giving, and sharing. Focusing only on ourselves does not bring us as much fulfillment and happiness as the joy of contributing to the greater good and helping others.

In her book, Cloé Madanes explains that the first four needs—certainty, variety, connection, and significance—are essential for human survival. These are the needs that the caring primal brain is constantly looking for quick and efficient ways to meet. "They are the fundamental needs of the personality—everyone must feel that they have met them on some level.

The last two needs—growth and contribution—Cloé Madanes considers to be essential for human fulfillment. "They are the needs of the spirit, and not everyone finds a way to satisfy them, although they are necessary for lasting fulfillment."[2]

Knowing the six human needs is necessary to be able to understand what drives your behavior and your child's behavior. However, merely knowing the needs is not going to help you connect with yourself or your child. You also need to understand how to meet your needs and support your child in meeting his needs in, as Madanes defines them, constructive rather than destructive ways.

The brain is already programmed to find ways to get our needs met. As discussed in Chapter 1, our primal brain looks for the most efficient, pleasant, and easy ways to meet our needs. The primal brain does not recognize, though, that the most efficient, pleasant, and easy ways to meet our needs are often destructive to our well-being and relationships. That is why the primal brain justifies any means as long as they help us survive by getting what it thinks we need. To distinguish between constructive and destructive ways of meeting our needs and find the constructive ways that best serve us, we need to engage our thinking brain.

Elijah's behavior was an example of his primal brain attempting to meet his needs in destructive ways. He did not intentionally choose those ways of meeting his needs. Elijah's primal brain made that choice for him. Doing the best he could with the resources he had, Elijah felt that those were the only ways that were available to him at that moment.

He was attempting to meet his need for significance in a

way that did not serve him by ignoring my invitation to get acquainted and refusing to follow the class routine (participating in the reading group). Throwing the shoe toward my group of students and me was another way of attempting to meet his need for significance ("Hey, I'm here. I want to be noticed. I matter.") and connection ("I feel lonely when I am by myself. I want to belong.") Deep inside, Elijah felt left out and wanted to join us, but he did not know how to do it in a constructive way.

I helped Elijah meet his need for significance by continuing to talk to him in a respectful and friendly way. I wanted him to be part of our group, regardless of how he behaved, so I agreed to read his book to the entire group. By inviting him to join the group and letting him know that he was still welcome to join, even after he threw his shoe, I helped Elijah meet his need for connection. Inviting him to join us was a message to him, "Regardless of how you behave, we understand that your behavior is not who you are, and we want you to be part of the group."

Understanding the six human needs also helped me make well-informed choices and not take Elijah's actions personally, which allowed me to keep my needs met. Instead of meeting my need for significance in a destructive way—by raising my voice, becoming demanding, or giving Elijah consequences to get him to treat me with respect, I reminded myself that my significance as a human being is inborn, as it is in every human, and that it was not defined by how others treated me.

In addition, instead of taking Elijah's behavior personally, I reminded myself that his intention was not to hurt anyone but to gain the feeling of security by using the ways that his brain had figured out were the most effective. Most likely, those ways of getting his needs met had worked for him in the past. As a result, I felt compassion and understanding and wanted to help.

As you can see, knowing the six human needs helped me

make better choices when handling the situation and allowed me to connect with Elijah by supporting both of us in constructively meeting our needs.

Understanding and Meeting Your Child's Needs

Certainty/Comfort/Security: The need to feel physically safe, emotionally secure, and certain is inherent in every human being. As you learned in Chapter 1, because the primal brain likes familiarity and predictability, it is afraid of and wants to move away or avoid the unknown. Therefore, to raise a self-sufficient, emotionally mature, and fulfilled child and build a strong, fully connected parent-child relationship, it is necessary to create a sense of trust and certainty in your relationship with your child.

In addition to feeling physically safe, the child needs to know that he is safe to come to you regardless of what he says or does. It is essential to distinguish between behavior and identity. The problem is never the child. It is him not yet knowing how to use his thinking brain to meet his needs in constructive ways.

Creating a safe place for your child to be vulnerable, be themselves, and be able to tell you the truth is not the same as excusing, justifying, supporting, or encouraging your child's inappropriate actions.

When seven-year-old Sadie admitted to her father that she was the one who stole the sticky note pad from her teacher's desk, Ryland felt the urge to immediately scold and shame Sadie. He wanted to tell her how embarrassed he felt and disappointed he was to have a daughter who was capable of stealing. Applying his knowledge of the six human needs helped him overcome that urge and understand that his little girl needed support from someone she could trust. Without his support, Sadie would not be able to change her behavior. Her honesty with her father was the first step toward her connection with herself and her father, so Ryland decided to focus on that first before moving on to any teaching.

Ryland said, "Sadie, I really appreciate you telling me the truth. It means a lot to me. I also know that that's not who you are (letting Sadie know that stealing was not an inherent part of her), and that it was something you did because there is more for you to learn about stealing and making better choices. I am happy to help you with that. Let's talk about what caused you to do what you did and then put our heads together to brainstorm how we can fix this situation and make sure it doesn't happen again."

In relief, Sadie smiled and cheerfully nodded her head.

The reason Sadie volunteered to share with Ryland what happened was that Ryland had been applying his knowledge of the six human needs to create a safe space for her in their relationship. By handling the stealing situation the way he did, Ryland strengthened Sadie's feelings of trust and safety with him. After this experience, Sadie is more likely to tell her father the truth and come to him for help in the future.

Let's compare this with another example. Ten-year-old Kamran stole his friend's brand-new fidget spinner. Based on his past experiences with his father, Dalmar, when he would get punished by doing wrong, Kamran was too intimidated to admit what he had done. Even though his father found the toy in Kamran's backpack after his teacher gave him a call, Kamran still denied stealing it. He did not feel safe admitting it to his father. Not because he was worried about his physical safety (Kamran was certain that his father would never hurt him physically), but his emotional safety. He was scared that if he told his father the truth, his father would put him down by saying things that would cause him to feel bad. If that happened, he would not know how to handle the feeling of embarrassment and being seen as "wrong." What Kamran feared the most was disconnecting from Dalmar by losing his father's love or being judged by him.

Kamran's primal brain wanted to protect him from that unpleasant experience. By denying stealing the toy, Kamran was still holding on to the possibility of his father understanding him and offering support instead of judging and criticizing Kamran for what he had done. Kamran was still holding on to the possibility of his need for love and connection being met.

Children are often aware of having done something wrong. Even when they may not be cognitively aware of it while doing it and act impulsively due to their primal brain's work, it is most likely that deep inside, they already feel bad about it. They may not show their regret or embarrassment for what they have done. Moreover, they may even attempt to intentionally create the façade of being indifferent and act as if they think there was nothing wrong with what they did. Trying to cause them to feel bad about what they have done in order to teach a lesson does not help either of you or your relationship. It may evoke resistance in the child that manifests itself as defensiveness or even aggression, which may lead to self-loathing.

Predictability in the way you respond to your child's misdeed helps your child feel secure, protected, and confident, especially if it is in a way that demonstrates that you are willing to hear your child out to understand him. It builds up his trust in you and desire to connect.

Creating a safe space for the child in a parent-child relationship does not mean that a parent has to react calmly and smile every time a child does something inappropriate. The parent may still express frustration or even anger. (We will talk more about expressing your feelings in Chapter 8.) Still, as long as the parent makes it clear to the child that she has those strong feelings about the child's action and not about who the child is, the child will trust the parent and feel safe around her.

Providing consistent schedules and routines is another way to help children feel confident and safe. As you already know, the human brain likes familiarity and consistency. It does not want to waste its energy on figuring out how to do new things every time or being uncertain about what's coming next. When it learns to do a certain activity at a certain time and in a certain way, it wants to stick with it so that it can be as efficient as possible. Having a routine helps the child improve their skills at doing certain tasks and procedures. Learning to be proficient at something creates competence.

When the child feels competent, he also feels confident and secure. That is why we see a toddler asking us to read him the same book over and over again or a teenager showing off by demonstrating the dance movements that she mastered through numerous repetitions. She feels confident and safe because she is sure that she probably won't make a mistake.

Significance: The word *significance* has a negative connotation for some people because of the destructive ways many people choose to meet this need. In this context, the need for significance is to simply know that "I matter," "I am being seen and heard," and "I am worthy."

Every person is already significant just by being a human. Even though significance is within us, we often do not feel that way. In children, this feeling of insignificance is often reinforced by the way their parents treat them. Having good intentions to help their child, some parents act controlling or bossy because they feel more competent and intelligent than their child. They disregard the child's opinion, forgetting that "a person's a person, no matter how small."[3]

Feeling unimportant, a child may begin making poor behavioral choices to meet their need for significance. Parents often see these choices as power struggles—the struggles between a parent and child to control the situation. A "power struggle" is one of the most harmful concepts that have become popularized in parenting.

As a Licensed Neuro-Linguistic Programming Practitioner with a Masters in Linguistics, I teach my clients to be very conscious of their chosen beliefs and the language they use. If you choose to believe that your child has a need for power, then the question that comes out of this belief is power over whom? Because if someone is in power, then there must be a person he is in power of. So, if your child wants power, then it means you are the one he wants to have power over. It further means that you may naturally feel resistance and will want to "regain" the power to meet *your* "need for power." Consequently, believing that a child has a need for power leads to tension and resistance in your parent-child relationship. Where there is tension and resistance, there is no connection.

The good news is that if you understand that it is not the need for power but the need for significance driving your child's behavior, you can avoid taking things personally. You can help your child meet this need in constructive ways, which will allow your child to connect with himself and you. Founder of Mary Kay Cosmetics, Inc., Mary Kay Ashe is known for saying, "Everyone has an invisible sign hanging from their neck saying, 'Make me feel important.'" Keeping that quote in mind has helped me numerous times to connect with children when they were exhibiting behavior that was difficult for me to deal with.

Seeing your child as important does not mean that you see him as more or less important than you or others, but as equally important. Understanding your child's need for significance excludes any comparison or feeling of superiority and evokes feelings of acceptance, compassion, and respect for your child and his needs.

The child may manifest his need for significance in destructive ways, such as sibling rivalry, competition, bullying, or other kinds of behavior that are difficult for parents to address that children often use to feel acknowledged, heard, or seen.

Angela, a single mother of three, used her understanding of her son Brian's need for significance to help him meet his need in a constructive way and to connect with her son in a situation that used to create conflict within the family.

When having dinner at the table with his mother and two older brothers, sixteen-year-old Dylan and eighteen-year-old Alex, eleven-year-old Brian would make sarcastic comments about others' remarks:

"I auditioned for the Christmas play today," said Dylan.

"Who cares?" Brian retorted.

"That's exciting!" said Angela.

"As exciting as my old socks are."

"Brian, could you please keep your comments to yourself?" Alex would interfere.

"What do you want from me? I'm not talking to you. Leave me alone."

Angela would remind Brian to be more respectful to his brothers. Still, he'd continue to seemingly purposely annoy his brothers until everyone would get frustrated with Brian's behavior, and he would get sent to his room.

This became a dinner "ritual" nobody looked forward to. It hurt Angela the most because she really wanted her children to get along. Instead, she witnessed them growing apart with each argument. Angela felt guilty about sending Brian to his room because she wanted him to feel part of the family. At the same time, she did not want the other boys to be treated disrespectfully.

When Angela learned about the six human needs, it became clear why Brian behaved the way he did. Although Angela had always been encouraging and loving with Brian, he still felt insignificant when he was around his older brothers. Because the older boys did most of the talking, it seemed like what was going on in their lives was more important. Angela realized that there were times when they would get caught up in discussing daily household matters and would forget to give Brian a chance to talk. Brian simply felt left out.

Upon realizing this, Angela suggested to the boys that they create a family rule at the dinner table: each family member would take a turn telling everyone about his or her day, and everyone else would listen attentively until the person was done sharing. Everyone would get about five minutes to share, and only afterward would they discuss household matters.

"It worked like magic," Angela shared with me. "I wish you could have seen Brian's face when we told him that it was his turn to tell us about his day, and all of us silently listened to him. He finally felt like he mattered. I wish I knew about human needs a long time ago. We could have avoided so many unpleasant feelings and arguments in our house."

Uncertainty/Variety: Finally, your child found something interesting to do. You are excited about having time to get some work done, and then take a minute just to sit down and relax. However, in a matter of minutes, he comes to find you to tell you that he's bored. You can forget about your relaxation time now!

It is believed in the field of child development that an average attention span is "3 to 5 minutes per year of a child's age."[4] It is especially true when children are doing a monotonous activity they are not interested in or something they feel they are forced to do. But what about the things that they like? As you probably noticed, they get bored or tired of things that they enjoy, too. That's because too much of everything and monotonous activity is tiring for the brain.

"What about video games?" Dale asked. "My nine-year-old son Calen would probably be playing them non-stop if I didn't set a limit. No boredom there." It definitely seems that way, but no worries! Video game developers took care of it! Even though it seems like playing video games is a monotonous activity, the process of playing video games provides variety for children. Children have access to a vast range of video games, difficulty levels in a game, characters to choose from, and various rewards and sounds.

Variety provides emotional stimulation. Different features and stages in a video game provide different levels of emotions —children go from anxious and worried about winning or achieving a goal to thrilled and delighted about getting what they want. Positive emotions increase dopamine levels in the brain and provide an emotional "high" that the primal brain keeps chasing.

Video game developers employ what is known about the human brain to make video games emotionally highly stimulating and entertaining for a young mind. When the child plays video games excessively, it becomes a destructive way of meeting the need for variety. Other examples of destructive ways the child may meet his needs include teasing his sibling or drawing on his bedroom wall when nobody is watching. You can help your child replace destructive ways of meeting his need for variety with constructive ones.

When Dale noticed that his son began having increasingly aggressive outbursts every time he was reminded that his video game playing time was up, he understood that Calen was meeting his need for variety in a destructive way because it was causing issues and could turn into an addiction. After learning about the six human needs, Dale decided to involve Calen in creating a Fun List. The list included different ways Calen could choose from to meet his need for variety constructively. The father and son had a lot of fun coming up with ideas together.

Calen's favorite became roughhousing with Dale. A couple of weeks later, Calen asked his father if they could have monthly brainstorming sessions to add new activities to the list. Calen began to spend much less time playing video games, and getting him off video games at the scheduled time has not been a problem for Dale anymore.

Love/Connection: With his demanding job, Oscar—the father of three-year-old Luke and six-year-old Mauricio — had to work from home on his computer after dinner while the boys played together. However, it was challenging for Oscar to get any work done because Luke would often disrupt him. "He finds every excuse to interrupt me," Oscar said with annoyance in his voice. "He comes up with different questions and problems or asks me to help with things that he can do by himself. I get nothing done."

"There is a reason why Luke acts that way. What do you think he needs from you?" I asked Oscar.

"Well, I think he just needs more time with me."

I explained to Oscar that wanting more time was not really what his children needed. Children don't need your time. They need your love. One of the strongest human needs is the need for love and connection. The Dalai Lama says, "Love and compassion are necessities, not luxuries. Without them, humanity cannot survive."

The need for love and connection for healthy human development and even survival is backed up by research. One of the first researchers, physician Henry Dwight Chapin, studied children who had been placed in ten orphanages and hospitals in New York in 1915. "These institutions provided an acceptable level of care in terms of hygiene and feeding, yet in nine of the ten all of the infants under two years old died."[5] In 1942, pediatrician Harry Bakwin proposed that the cause of high infant death rates was "emotional deprivation."[6]

Studies by other researchers, such as Lawson Lowrey, William Goldfarb, Rene Spitz, John Bowlby, and Charles Nelson, also found that children in orphanages and foster homes under age five were demonstrating high instances of mental, emotional, and physical health issues and developmental delays along with high infant death rates, which the researchers attributed to a lack of physical and emotional contact.[7] [8] [9]

The next time we met, Oscar shared with me that when he was working again, Luke came up and began pressing the computer buttons. Oscar asked him to play with Mauricio a few times, but Luke would keep pressing buttons. Oscar finally lost it and pushed Luke's hand away. As soon as he did so, Oscar realized what he had done and felt terrible. He immediately turned to Luke to apologize. How surprised Oscar was to see Luke looking back with a smile—his father was finally present with him. That was the moment when Oscar remembered that Luke was not trying to be annoying or difficult. All his son was doing was using the way he hoped would work to connect with his father to meet his need for love and connection.

Oscar hugged his son, acknowledged that Luke wanted to play, and reassured him that they would play when he finished his work. Knowing that he could count on his need for love and connection being met, Luke stopped interrupting his father. When Oscar was done with his work, the family had a wonderful time playing together.

That night, Oscar decided that he would spend at least thirty minutes connecting with his boys before sitting down to work on his computer. That small change had a substantial beneficial effect on the lives of all three of them. The boys knew that they could count on their need for love and connection being met.

Growth/Self-actualization: Everything in life either evolves, grows, and improves, or regresses, decreases, and declines. The concept of self-actualization was initially introduced by a German neurologist and psychiatrist Kurt Goldstein and popularized by Maslow in his hierarchy of needs theory. According to Maslow, self-actualization is "the full realization of one's potential."[10] [11] Every human has the need for self-actualization, the need to fully express "one's true self."[12] Therefore, it is of utmost importance for a child's need for self-actualization to be met in order to feel fulfilled and have a meaningful life.

The process of self-actualization is different for every child. For example, some children may self-actualize themselves through dancing, painting, or writing. Others may self-actualize through finding unique and innovative ways of solving problems or learning software programming.

Self-actualization is a bilateral process of becoming the best version of yourself while staying true to your ever-evolving self. On the one hand, it is a child discovering his true self and capabilities by connecting with himself. On the other hand, he is becoming the best he can be and developing a stronger character by learning new skills, growing and challenging himself, and overcoming life challenges.

It is essential to keep in mind that the parents' job is not to force their children to self-actualize and reach their full potential, which parents often do by forcing their children to participate in extracurricular activities that the children may not even like. Parents' mission is to encourage and inspire their child to challenge himself in the areas of his interest, provide guidance in his choosing, and support him on the journey of his choice.

Contribution: We all have the need to contribute. Contributing is a higher form of giving. It is adding value to someone else's life. For a child, it could mean contributing to relationships with the people who are close to him—

caregivers, family members, and close friends—and contributing to the family as a whole.

"Wait a minute!" I often get from confused parents. "How is my five-year-old son supposed to contribute to our family? It's not like he has a job or can do things that adults can do, like cook a meal for the family, fix a broken chair, or clean the house by himself."

Yes, that is true. A child may not be able to contribute to a family to the same degree that parents can. However, that does not mean that there are no meaningful ways he can contribute to the family. Your child wants to feel part of something bigger—either the family or his relationship with you—which adds more meaning to his life. Humans feel genuinely fulfilled when they contribute to a bigger purpose and collective well-being. Our need to give is greater than our need to take. Therefore, your child will feel more worthy, joyful, and fulfilled when he is able to contribute in a meaningful way.

While a child may not be physically and developmentally ready yet to cook a meal for the family independently, he may contribute to the shared cause by unpacking or washing ingredients for you. While a child may not be ready to fix a broken chair, he may help you by handing tools to you. While a child may not be ready to clean a house by himself, he may be ready to do the easiest house chores independently or with you by his side.

Parents who help their children meet their need for contribution in constructive ways help their child increase their self-esteem, independence, and sense of responsibility. They also help the child recognize himself as a valuable member of the family and society. In addition, parents make their own lives easier.

Learning about the need to contribute helped Banee realize how she was robbing her seven-year-old daughter Mingmei of the opportunity to meet her need for contribution. "I would try to do everything for Mingmei. I would clear the table after her. I would organize her toys for her. I would tell her to just go and play when she would ask if she could help me fold laundry. No wonder she would continue spilling things, making a mess, and never picking up after herself."

Banee shared, "It's different now. I don't do anything Mingmei can do for herself. She knows that taking care of her own things is her way of contributing. She also contributes to our family by helping me with feeding the fish, laundry, and grocery shopping. Mingmei is a different person now. I can't believe how mature, responsible, and caring she has become."

Understanding human needs will help you see your child and his behavior choices more objectively. Empowered with this knowledge, you will also be able to help your child meet his needs in constructive ways by strengthening his connection with himself and your connection with him. As you do so, I want to help you avoid a common mistake that I see parents make again and again. Turn the page to learn what you can do to avoid this mistake and ensure that you and your child have the lives you deserve.

Your Child's Needs
Action Step

Use your *Parenting Connection Workbook* to access a chart that explores the constructive and destructive ways that your child attempts to meet his needs. This activity will help you and your child find better ways to meet his needs. Visit www. albinspire.com/workbook to download your copy.

4

WHAT ABOUT YOUR NEEDS?

There is a reason why on an airplane, they ask you to be sure to adjust your own mask before helping others, including your child. Although it may seem selfish, you know that not taking care of yourself first may be fatal for you and your child. Just like on an airplane, the same applies to your everyday life. Not taking care of your own needs first may be harmful to you and your child and lead to you taking actions that are damaging to your parent-child relationship and connection.

You cannot give what you do not have. One of the biggest common mistakes parents make is that they often become so focused on meeting the child's needs that they forget there is a reason why those needs are called "human needs," not "child's needs." Just like your child, you are a human, and you need to ensure that your needs are met before you attempt to meet her needs.

Does this seem selfish? Think about all the adults you meet in your life who blame and resent their parents, despite recognizing that their parents sacrificed a lot to ensure their happiness. Why? It is because those parents put their needs aside and made their children's needs the focus of their entire lives. When you ignore your needs, you don't feel fulfilled or happy, and your children will sense it. When they do, they will not feel fulfilled or happy either.

Sooner or later, you burn out, grow resentful, or have moments when you snap and take it out on your children. Not meeting your needs may also lead to unconscious manipulation of your children. You may think, "How can you treat me like this after all I have done for you?" Your children may feel guilty for all you do for them at the cost of your own happiness. That definitely does not foster a connection in your parent-child relationship.

Meeting Your Needs

Certainty/Comfort/Security: For some parents, just knowing that food will be on the table tomorrow or that they will get a paycheck at the end of the week or month is enough to meet their need for certainty. For others, meeting their need for certainty requires having a certain amount of money in their bank account or a big beach house for their family. It is different for everyone. There is no right or wrong with needing what you need to feel certain and safe as long as it works for you and you meet this need in a constructive way—a way that serves you and your child and does not harm anyone.

Meeting their need for certainty in a parent-child relationship for some parents simply means trusting that their child is safe and making the right choices when on her own. The destructive way of meeting the need for certainty would be parents needing their child to be next to them in order to be able to control the child's actions to make sure that the child does "the right thing" all the time. Consciously or subconsciously choosing to meet their needs in destructive ways, parents may end up damaging their and the child's emotional, mental, or physical wellbeing.

Monica used to be one of those parents who constantly

needed to know where their child was in order to meet her need for certainty. Whenever her 11-year-old son Kevin visited his friend Freddie, she would call her son, Freddie, or Freddie's mother, Sofia, every half an hour to check on Kevin. As a result, Kevin would feel annoyed and controlled. He would become upset with his mother, and their relationship began deteriorating. Kevin's relationship with Freddie also became worse because Freddie began making fun of Kevin and calling him a "momma's boy."

Embarrassed and resentful, Kevin would start a fight with Freddie, which would only reinforce Monica's insecurities and prove that she did have a reason to worry and check on Kevin, without realizing that, unintentionally, she was the one whose actions caused the boys' fighting. In addition, Monica's relationship with Sofia worsened. Sofia felt untrusted by Monica and thought of as incapable of taking care of the children.

After our work together, Monica realized that she was meeting her need for certainty in a destructive way and needed to find a constructive way if she wanted these relationships to improve. Monica promised Sofia, Freddie, and Kevin not to call them anymore, but instead trust them to give her a call as soon as they felt unsafe or needed help. She began working on decreasing her anxiety and creating a feeling of certainty when Kevin wasn't around by using the Parenting Success Formula you will learn about in the next chapter and imagining how much fun her son was having. This change improved Monica's relationships with all of them and strengthened the boy's friendship. It also helped Kevin feel trusted by his mother, which led to a stronger connection between the two.

Uncertainty/Variety: Remember a monotonous or repetitive task you recently performed? You may have noticed that your body and mind got tired, even if the task was not particularly taxing. That is what happens when we do not have variety. Sometimes we get bored even by the things that we usually enjoy doing, such as watching TV, listening to our favorite kind of music, or spending time with children when we do those things often or for a prolonged period.

When we become physically and emotionally tired and bored, we naturally want to change the activity and do something different in order to feel excited or rejuvenated. Variety helps us feel alive. Just like with any other need, parents can meet this need in a constructive or destructive way. To meet your need for variety in a constructive way, you could hire a babysitter or ask a friend or family member to watch your child so that you can give yourself some time to recharge by doing activities you like. Some parents meet their need for variety by going out with friends or taking a trip. Others prefer spending time alone and relaxing.

Meeting their need for variety in destructive ways serves neither parents nor their child. Some examples are activities such as excessive drinking, compulsive shopping, or spending too much time using social media. An interesting point that Cloé Madanes makes is that some people satisfy their need for uncertainty by creating problems. It is especially true when things are going well. People get used to how things are, begin taking things for granted, and as a result, feel bored. Looking for the feeling of excitement that uncertainty and variety bring, they subconsciously create problems.[1]

My client Yazmin unconsciously did this by fearing that the things that were going well wouldn't last. Yazmin's thirteen-year-old son Sahil was doing really well in school. He participated in extracurricular activities, enjoyed learning, and was respected by his classmates. Instead of feeling excited about her son doing well, Yazmin would feel more worried and stressed with each advancing year.

She would spend many nights awake worrying about what

would happen if Sahil lost his interest in learning or if the following year's academic standards became too hard for him. Seeing his mother so anxious all of the time caused Sahil to become worried about his mother and focus on her emotional state rather than on his academics, which resulted in a decline in his sleep quality, energy level, and grades.

Yazmin's fear had become a self-fulfilling prophecy that began affecting the quality of her and her son's life. Being worried about each other, the mother and the son began avoiding talking about their feelings and concerns to avoid causing the other to feel more worry or stress, which led to the weakening of the connection between them.

After learning about her needs, Yazmin chose to make meeting her own needs a priority in order to be able to be in the best emotional state she could be. She decided to live in the present, celebrate her son's successes, and stop trying to predict the future. Implementing much of what I share in this book helped her to feel calmer, improve her health, and strengthen the connection between her and her son.

Significance: Parents meet their need for significance in various ways, from constructive ways, such as providing for their family and working on personal and professional development to destructive ways, such as putting their children down or attempting to control their children. Unfortunately, parents who use destructive ways to meet their need for significance often do not realize the real reason for, and the cost behind, their actions.

Naturally wanting to meet their need for significance from feeling respected and listened to by their child, they unwittingly cause their child's emotional suffering and lower the child's sense of self-worth, which weakens the connection and destroys the feeling of trust in their parent-child relationship. "If only your aunt saw what a spoiled brat you are and how you talk to me after all I have done for you, she would never bring you any gifts anymore. She would not even want to come over and see you again!"

It can be extremely challenging for parents to notice and recognize these unhealthy patterns of behavior. That is why many of the families I work with invite me for a home visit so that they can gain more awareness about their unhealthy patterns of behavior in their parent-child relationship by receiving objective, professional feedback. Only when parents are aware can they make the changes they want.

Some parents may get so used to running the unconscious patterns that even when they begin noticing their destructive patterns, they have a hard time admitting to themselves, let alone to someone else, that that behavior is destructive. This is because they are embarrassed about their actions. They want to change their behavior, but either don't know how or find it very challenging. So, their primal brain often looks for an easier "solution" to this problem; it justifies their behavior with logical and rational explanations instead of going through the inconvenience of changing it: "I yelled at her because I want her to stop talking to me that way."

It seems like it makes sense, but when parents give it more thought, they understand that they are attempting to fix their child's behavior in destructive ways. It is vital for parents to be honest with themselves and objectively reflect on their behavior, not to find out what is "wrong" with themselves, but to understand how their behavior helps them meet their needs and whether it is the way they want to continue to behave.

Two signs that you may be meeting your need for significance in a destructive way is if you feel like you have to justify your behavior or when you are using one of the following ways to get your child do what you want: criticizing, belittling, manipulating the child, lying to your child, abusing your child emotionally or physically, making comments that have the potential to cause the child to feel guilty or less worthy, putting the child down, yelling at your child, bribing, or threatening your child.

Frequently, when I share with parents some of the destructive parenting approaches to meeting the need for significance, they immediately respond, "Oh, that's not me. I don't do that." That was Gabrielle's reaction. She invited me for a home visit to observe her and her seven-year-old daughter, Debricka. Gabrielle asked Debricka to put her toys away and go brush her teeth before going to bed.

"Just a second," replied Debricka from the playroom, "I'm putting my Barbie's dress on her."

"Debricka, I want you to stop right now and do what I asked you to do," Gabrielle shouted back.

"Why?"

"Because I said so," Gabrielle said in a frustrated voice.

After the home visit, I asked Gabrielle, "What was your reason for not allowing Debricka to finish dressing her Barbie doll?"

"Because she didn't listen to me. "

"Debricka did not say she was not going to put away the toys. What would have changed if you had allowed her to finish dressing her Barbie first?"

"Well," said Gabrielle. "Nothing, I guess."

"Do you think she would still clean up the toys and go brush her teeth?"

"I think so. She's used to that routine."

"There was no sign of Debricka refusing to listen to you. It looked like she wanted to complete what she was already doing first."

I then asked Gabrielle to think about what need she was trying to meet. She realized she was trying to meet her need for significance but was doing so in a way that she previously said she'd never done—by trying to control her daughter. Gabrielle looked embarrassed, but I encouraged her not to be and, instead, celebrate becoming aware of what she has been doing. While she could not change the past, she was now empowered to change her future by finding constructive ways to meet her need for significance.

Gabrielle is not alone. Many parents use destructive ways to meet their need for significance. Unless parents become aware of their behavior and work on consciously choosing constructive ways of meeting their need for significance, they will continue running down the same path of unhealthy parent-child relationships by weakening their connection with the child.

Love/Connection: Although love and connection are prerequisites for building a healthy parent-child relationship, parents need to be conscious about the ways they meet their need for love and connection in the relationship with their child. That is because depending on your choices, you can either become more connected with or alienate your child. For example, you can meet your need for love and connection in a constructive way by connecting with your child through conversations, hugging, and sharing your feelings.

Alternatively, you can meet this need in destructive ways by insisting your child connect with you through the way that works for you without being considerate of whether it works for your child. For example, parents who do not consider or respect their children's preferences and needs regarding physical affection may leave the child with the impression that they are selfish, controlling, and needy, rather than loving and affectionate. This is something that happened in twelve-year-old Mona's life.

Her mother, Jiya, did not have loving connections with her parents when she was a child and felt unlovable. When Jiya decided to have a child, she promised herself that she will build a relationship with her child, in which both will always feel loved and connected. It was Jiya's way to make up for what she did not have and ensure that her daughter doesn't go through the emotionally painful experience that she went through as a child. In fulfilling her promise, Jiya unintentionally chose a destructive way of meeting her need for love and connection. She would insist on her daughter talking to her about her feelings and the reason she felt that way every time Jiya noticed that Mona looked sad, even in instances when Mona did not feel like talking about what happened or sharing her feelings.

Consequently, Mona would withdraw and try to avoid conversations with her mother completely. Such behavior would cause Jiya to feel hurt, untrusted, and unloved. She would accuse her daughter of being insensitive and unloving. The mother and daughter grew resentful toward each other and considered the other selfish and inconsiderate.

When Jiya realized that she unwittingly had chosen to use a destructive way to meet her need for love and connection, she decided to replace it with a constructive one. She told Mona that she loved, cared for, and trusted her and that she was not going to demand her daughter to share with her when Jiya wanted it, but when Mona felt like it. That approach gave Mona some space and gave Jiya an opportunity to practice loving her daughter and feeling connected with her even in the moments when her daughter was not sharing with her.

Another way parents meet their need for love and connection is by pleasing their children and giving in to the child's every whim. Parents often mistake their child-pleasing behavior as unconditional love because they both may look similar from the outside. The way to distinguish between the two is by connecting with yourself to identify how you feel. When it is truly unconditional love, you feel light and joyful. It does not feel like a sacrifice. You expect absolutely nothing in return from your child. If you find yourself hoping that if you do everything you *think* your child wants you to do, your child will love you more, then you need to be aware of it. This is nothing more than an unhealthy and destructive way of meeting your need for love and connection through child pleasing.

All this type of behavior does is turn a parent-child relationship into a trade, in which both sides suffer. The parent suffers because she often feels unappreciated and taken for granted. The child also suffers because her parent's behavior feels like a burden to her. If the parent does too much for the child based on guessing what the child might want or need and without the child asking her, the child may feel annoyed, controlled, or having to feel grateful when she doesn't really care about or need what is done for her. If the parent does everything the child wants her to do and then reminds the child what she has done for her when she doesn't listen to her or does not show or express gratitude, the child may feel manipulated.

Additionally, exclusively focusing on pleasing your child to get more of her love unwittingly teaches her to use love to subconsciously manipulate others. She learns that she can tell her parents, "I love you if you do this for me," to get what she wants. Getting everything she wants also teaches her that she does not have to put time or effort into earning it. Becoming used to hearing "yes" all the time and getting what she wants, she learns to expect certain things and actions from her parents and take things for granted. If one day she hears "no," she is going to blame the parents for not providing her with what she wants.

When it comes to meeting the need for love and connection, I want to assure you that you don't need to worry about love and connection disappearing in your parent-child relationship. I have witnessed time and time again that a child's love and desire for connection with her parents are always there, even when she acts as if or says that she does not care about, love, or need her parents. Deep inside, she knows that's not true.

Children are born with a need for love and connection, and you as the primary caregiver are the main source of both for them. I have seen cases where parents would be considered "terrible" by social standards for physically and emotionally abusing their children, but their children still craved their love as well as physical and emotional connection with them.

I will never forget working with fifth-grader Owen. He was known at school as "one of the students with severe behavior issues." He would do anything, including physically attacking other students and staff, just to be sent home. His desire to leave school and go home did not make sense to most adults in the building because everyone treated him nicely—completely opposite to how he was treated at home. His mother would make derogatory comments, call him names, physically punish him, and spend most of the time depressed in her room while leaving Owen on his own. It would seem to make more sense for Owen to want to be at school, around people who loved him and wanted to connect with him. It would, but not to Owen. Behind his seemingly illogical actions laid the strong, genuine, and natural need for love for and from the person whose love and connection he craved the most. Just being in the same apartment as his mother was meeting his need for love and connection more than being loved and cared for by all the adults and friends in the school. That is how powerful the child's love and connection to you is.

Never be afraid of your child not loving you because you say "no" to her. If you do it in a respectful and calm manner, coming from a place of unconditional love, your child will respect and understand your choice. She might not like it, especially if she is used to you saying "yes" to everything, but she will learn to accept and eventually understand that your "no" had nothing to do with your love for her and was for the good of both of you.

. . .

Growth: Everything in nature either grows or dies. As humans, we have the need to develop, evolve, and grow. When we stop growing, we degenerate, regress, or weaken.

One may disagree, "But we also have a third option: staying still and not moving." That's not really an option. When you think you choose to remain where you are, what you really choose is to regress. Think about what happens with a muscle when it's not being used for a long time. It atrophies —it loses its muscle tissue. Muscle atrophy leads to muscle weakness, proneness to injury, and may cause disability.

The same is true about the connection in your parent-child relationship. You either take action to strengthen your connection, or your connection gradually weakens when you do not put in effort into strengthening it. There are numerous ways you can grow as a human and role model for your child —you can choose your own way of growth—whether it is growing intellectually, professionally, spiritually, or advancing your parenting skills. Continuous learning is one of the best ways the parents I work with choose to help themselves grow. You reading my book right now is one of your ways to meet your need for growth.

The ways and the extent to which parents choose to grow depend on many factors, including their values, past experiences, the goals they have in life, and their willingness to tolerate the discomfort that comes with stepping out of their comfort zone and learning to apply a new skill that can be challenging. I have worked with parents who have found ways to grow anywhere from exercising for twenty minutes a day and watching a short video on parenting to running three marathons and getting an M.A. degree in less than two years while taking care of little children and working full-time. There is no right or wrong way to grow—everyone has to decide for themselves what they want to create in their lives and choose a constructive way that feels right for them.

. . .

Contribution: It is human nature to want to give, help others, and make the world a better place, especially when it is the world of a loved one. That is why contributing to their child's world is often the most joyful and rewarding aspect of parenting. It is also constructive as long as it does not turn into the parent's single point of focus and impede the child's personal growth. Contributing to their child's world is what helps many parents feel fulfilled and live a meaningful life.

Parents may choose to meet their need for contribution by teaching their child to use kitchen utensils, helping them with homework, or investing in their children's education. Parents may also choose to involve other professionals and adults to support them in contributing to the child's growth and help the child learn the necessary skills that will become the foundation for developing healthy relationships with people in her life.

Parents may also meet their need for contribution through ways that are not related to parenting. Regardless of where we are in our lives right now, what we have, and how much money we earn, we can always find something to give—it may be money, time, or effort. For instance, some of my clients choose to contribute by making financial donations to a charity, while others prefer volunteering their time at organizations that support people with depression or addiction issues.

A client of mine, Quiana, found her way of contributing by brightening other peoples' worlds. Quiana made a Contribution Tradition for herself. She committed to making a daily act of kindness for others, like letting someone go in front of her in a line at the grocery store, opening the door for someone, or simply listening attentively after asking someone how they were doing that day. Those small acts of contributing to another's world inspired not only her, but also her children, to do more for others.

It's incredible how easy contributing can be. Sometimes, a

kind word or a sincere, cheerful smile to a passerby may be one of the easiest ways of meeting your need for contribution.

In addition to understanding how your brain and your child's brain work, you now know how to meet your needs and help your child meet her needs in constructive ways. In the next chapter, you will learn how you can create lasting results in your parent-child relationship by using one of the most powerful parenting tools—the Parenting Success Formula.

What About Your Needs?
Action Step

Go to your *Parenting Connection Workbook* to identify the ways that you attempt to meet your needs so that you can make more purposeful decisions when choosing ways to meet your needs. Visit www.albinspire.com/workbook to download your copy.

PART II

THE PARENTING SUCCESS FORMULA

5

THE PARENTING SUCCESS FORMULA

Closely watching her parents' reaction, six-year-old birthday girl Madison dips her finger in the frosting on the cake, brings it to her lips, and begins licking it while making loud smacking noises. Madison knows that it is considered impolite. Despite knowing this, with so many guests at the party, she decides to use the opportunity to avoid getting in trouble. She knows Mommy and Daddy will say nothing when there are people around.

Her father, James, notices it and does not like it. He really wants to intervene but turns around and continues to carry on with his conversation.

Patricia, Madison's mother, is attempting to follow suit, but it is extremely challenging. Her eyes keep turning to Madison. Madison notices the look, but the pleasure of finally having a chance to do what she wants and not what she has been told to do is too irresistible to her primal brain, so she continues dipping her finger into the frosting and then deliciously and loudly enjoying it.

Finally, Patricia cannot take it anymore, "That is enough, young lady!" Patricia explodes, "That's disgusting! Get up right now and go wash your hands." The cheerful conversation at the birthday table ceases for a moment. Everyone involuntarily looks at Madison and her mother. They both look embarrassed. To spare them from embarrassment, the guests get back to socializing, pretending like they have not witnessed anything.

Why did the two parents react to the exact same situation differently? They both felt embarrassed by their daughter's behavior. They both wanted her to stop. They both shared the same values. Yet, the action each of them took was different. Despite the situation being the same, the way they *thought* about the situation was different.

When James noticed Madison eating the cake with her fingers, he felt irritated and embarrassed. After realizing that intervening could have cost him more embarrassment, he decided to allow his daughter to continue behaving that way by thinking to himself, "I sure hope my friends don't notice Madison's behavior. If they do, we'll definitely lose our reputation as good parents. Seeing her do that is just intolerable. I better ignore her and keep our guests distracted."

When Patricia saw Madison eating with her fingers, she thought, "What an embarrassment! She knows not to eat with her fingers! She clearly sees that I'm not happy about that, yet keeps doing it. I can't believe how disrespectful she is!"

What James and Patricia did not know was that the language we use in our heads to interpret situations and events in our lives affects the way we feel, and the way we feel affects the actions we take. The way James thought about the situation caused him to question his "goodness" as a parent and worry about his reputation. As a result, his response to the situation was to ignore his daughter's behavior, along with his feelings about it, and distract himself from his thoughts by distracting his guests from the incident.

Patricia's way of thinking, on the other hand, caused her

frustration. Not being able to contain her emotions any longer, she began shouting at her daughter in front of everyone.

By thinking differently about the same situation, each parent felt differently, and because they felt differently, they took different actions. By taking different actions, the parents achieved different outcomes, but neither got the results they were hoping for because of the way they were thinking.

The good news is that because our thinking affects the results we get, we have the power to choose the thoughts we want to think, and thus, the ability to get the results we want.

Many parents often think that significant changes in their child's behavior and their parent-child relationship require massive action, which is usually not the case. Did you know that if a pilot flying from Los Angeles to New York city shifts the route by just 3.5 degrees south, the airplane will end up in Washington, D.C. instead of New York?[1] What a huge difference a tiny shift can make! The same is true about the big changes you can make as a parent by slightly shifting the route of your thinking. As the co-founder of Neuro-Linguistic Programming (NLP) Richard Bandler said at his NLP Practitioner international training that I attended, "If you change the way you think, you will change the way you feel, and, therefore, you will change the way you act." When you change the way you act, you will get different results.

I have put this into an easy-to-memorize formula, which I call the Parenting Success Formula, to help parents and their children use their thinking purposefully in order to create the fully connected parent-child relationships they deserve. I teach my clients the life-changing Parenting Success Formula with joy, enthusiasm, and confidence—because it works. Knowing how to apply this formula to your daily parenting will help you make the desired changes in your parent-child relationship.

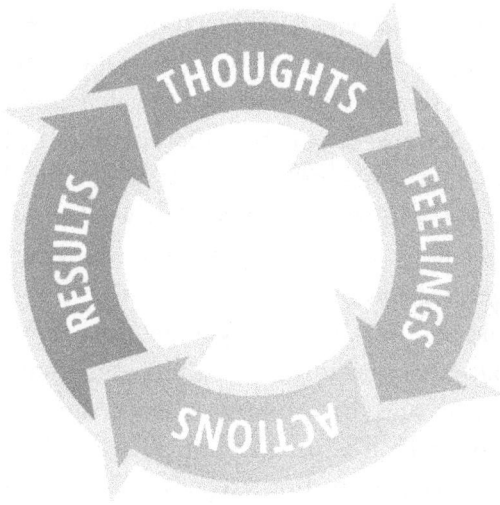

This concept is not new to humanity. This is the truth that many thought and spiritual leaders have come to realize through generations. Way back in Ancient Greece, Plato stated, "Reality is created by the mind. We can change our reality by changing our mind." Buddha said, "Our life is shaped by our mind; we become what we think."

Learning to Think Differently

As a loving mother, Patricia had positive intent—she wanted her daughter to use her manners. Patricia also wanted the guests to like her daughter, recognize that Madison's parents had taken time and effort to teach their daughter good manners, and enjoy their meal instead of, in Patricia's mind, being disgusted by the socially inappropriate way Madison was eating. Patricia's thinking, though, did not help her achieve the result she wanted. Instead of helping her daughter make better decisions by connecting with her, Patricia ended up weakening the connection between her and Madison. She did not take time to connect with herself first so that she could take action from a loving place.

James's way of going about the situation did not help him connect with Madison either. Moreover, he missed the opportunity to connect with himself. Instead of choosing to act with integrity and help his daughter make better choices, he chose to ignore her behavior by distracting himself and his guests.

Unknowingly, many parents make the same mistakes. They have simply never been taught how to use the most powerful tool on the planet—the brain—in a manner that allows them to design their thinking in ways that would help them achieve the results that would best serve their children and themselves. Developing the skill of using their brain to think consciously and purposefully allows parents to teach their children and help them avoid making the same mistakes due to running the harmful, programmed belief systems.

Mastering Metacognition

Since our thoughts affect our actions and, ultimately, the results we get in life, in order to construct the life we want, we need to develop strong metacognitive skills. The word "metacognition" derives from a Greek prefix "meta," meaning "beyond," and from a Latin word "cognitio," meaning "knowledge." Thus, metacognition means going beyond just knowing. It is thinking about what you know and are aware of, so that you can analyze, reflect on, and orchestrate your thinking. It is that voice inside your head that says things such as, "Where are my keys? I always put them here. Hmm…Let me think…The last time I saw them was when…"

Metacognition is "talking" with yourself about your thinking, the challenges you encounter, and the choices you can make to solve those challenges. Metacognition is made possible due to our highly developed thinking brain. It empowers us to change our thoughts by choosing the thoughts that serve us and bring us closer to the desired result.

To develop strong metacognitive skills, the first step you need to take is to bring your unconscious thoughts to your awareness. You cannot change what you are not aware of. Imagine you invited your friend over for dinner. As you are both enjoying the meal, some lettuce gets stuck in your teeth. You can't see or feel it. Unless your friend notices and points it out to you, you will continue eating and talking without being aware that it's there. When your friend points it out to you, though, you gain the power of awareness. What is powerful about awareness? Now you get to consciously choose what to do about the lettuce stuck in your teeth and how to do it: you can leave it there until you are done eating or take it out; you can take it out with a toothpick or by brushing your teeth. You get to decide.

The same is true about your thinking: once you become aware of your thoughts, the results you are getting in your life will no longer be at the mercy of your unconscious programming. You will get to decide whether you want to keep thinking those old programmed thoughts or replace them with thoughts that better serve you.

Creating Space to Connect

To become aware of your thoughts, you need to connect with yourself first. Austrian neurologist, psychiatrist, and Holocaust survivor Viktor Frankl said: "Between stimulus and response there is a space. In that space is our power to choose our response. In our response lies our growth and our freedom."[2] Regardless of how stressful a situation or event is, you can always remind yourself that you do not have to react to it instantly.

Instead, step back and allow yourself to take that space between the stimulus (the situation or event) and your response in order to connect with yourself to become aware of your feelings and thoughts. You can then consciously decide how you want to respond. Use that space to take responsibility for the action you are about to take.

Notice that the word *responsibility* encompasses the words that describe its meaning, *response* and *ability*—it is your ability to consciously respond—not react—to a situation. Only you get to decide how you want to respond to achieve the results you want.

Parenting Success Formula

When hearing about the Parenting Success Formula, some parents who are not familiar with my work assume that it is all about positive thinking. It's not quite so. The purpose of the Parenting Success Formula is not to distract, avoid, or blindly deny an issue by thinking positively about it, but to connect with yourself in order to be able to handle the issue from a loving, peaceful, and compassionate place rather than from a place of panic and fear created by your primal brain. In the state of being connected to yourself, you can take a conscious action based on your values and rational thinking and focus on developing connection in your parent-child relationship.

Here is the five-step process of the Parenting Success Formula:

Step 1. Become Aware of the Feeling

Take that space between the stimulus and your response to become aware of what you feel by asking yourself, "What am I feeling right now?" Name the feeling and allow yourself to feel it without avoiding, judging, or resisting it. Naming the feeling has two functions. One, it helps you tune into your body and, two, it allows you to calm down. Research shows that by having the left logical, "linguist expert" part of the brain name the feeling generated in the emotional brain causes it to release neurotransmitters down to the right limbic area in the emotional brain and calm it down.[3] Dan Siegel calls this approach "Name It to Tame It."[4]

Step 2. Become Aware of Your Thoughts

Once you have become aware of your feeling, investigate what thoughts caused it by asking yourself, "What am I thinking right now? What are the thoughts I am having that are creating this feeling?" For the formula to be effective, you must be completely honest with yourself when answering this question and shine a light on everything you think.

It is common for parents not to like their thoughts about the situation or their child when their emotions run high, so they begin feeling guilty, judging themselves, or trying to filter their thoughts. This step is not for you to judge yourself for having these thoughts. This step is to reveal every thought you have without associating it with who you are. Your thoughts are not you. You need to see them for what they are—simply thoughts in your mind.

Step 3. Evaluate Your Thoughts

When you become aware of your thoughts, you have an opportunity to consciously evaluate them. Notice that I intentionally did not use "judge." When you judge your thoughts, you label them as good or bad. If you label them as bad, you often begin judging yourself as bad for thinking those thoughts.

Evaluate the thoughts instead, which means draw conclusions from closely examining your thoughts. Ask yourself, "Does thinking these thoughts cause me to respond in a way that will help me connect with my child?" If the answer is "yes," you can choose to keep thinking those thoughts. If the answer is "no," you have an opportunity to choose different thoughts that will help you achieve the desired result by connecting with yourself and your child.

Step 4. Decide What You Want to Think

Contemplate what thoughts you could be thinking instead that would help you create an emotion that would encourage you to respond in a way that would serve both you and your child and help you connect. Ask yourself, "What thoughts would help me feel more compassionate, calm, and understanding?"

Step 5. Practice Thinking New Thoughts

Thinking those thoughts may feel unusual at first and require effort. However, practicing thinking them over and over again will physically change your brain by creating new, strong neural pathways in it. Eventually, your new way of thinking will become subconscious. You will begin noticing how you parent differently, in a more connected way.

The Role of Purposeful Responses in the Parenting Success Formula

When explaining the Parenting Success Formula to families I work with, I use the word "response" and not "reaction" for a reason. A reaction is an action that you usually take unconsciously and spontaneously, without much consideration and contemplation about how it will impact you, others, or the result you want to achieve. That is why a more accurate name for the Fight, Flight, or Freeze *response* would be the Fight, Flight, or Freeze *reaction*. When you are reacting, that is how you know that you are weakening the connection with your child by not applying the Parenting Success Formula, which requires you to pause and take space to connect with yourself first in order to choose a conscious and purposeful response.

Let's see how Patricia and James could have achieved different results if only they knew and implemented the four steps of the Parenting Success Formula.

Patricia:

1. **Become Aware of the Feeling.** Patricia could take the space to become aware of her feelings by asking herself, "What am I feeling right now?" Naming the feeling ("I feel angry.") would help Patricia connect with herself and calm down a little.

2. **Become Aware of Your Thoughts.** Then, Patricia could ask herself, "What am I thinking right now? What are the thoughts I am having that are creating this feeling?" "I think that my daughter is embarrassing us. Our guests are going to think that we're bad parents because we haven't taught her how to use her table manners. I also think that she's being disrespectful to her father and me. I think that she doesn't care about how we feel or what our guests think. If she continues this way, she will grow into a selfish, disrespectful, and inconsiderate person who will use any means necessary to get what she wants and not care about anyone else."

3. **Evaluate Your Thoughts.** Now that Patricia has become aware of her thoughts, she could consciously evaluate them by asking herself, "Is thinking like this going to cause me to respond in the way that will help me connect with Madison?" Asking this question would help her realize that continuing to think this way would prevent her from responding in a way that would serve her in achieving the

desired result—to help Madison realize how her inappropriate behavior could be affecting others and guide her daughter in making better choices.

4. **Decide What You Want to Think.** Based on her realization, Patricia could have decided to choose different thoughts that would help her connect with herself and her daughter. For example, she could have chosen to think, "I know that my husband and I are good parents and that we have taught our daughter to use good table manners. She's choosing not to right now because she is excited about the opportunity to eat in a more fun way. It doesn't mean that she disrespects us. She might not even realize that I'm embarrassed. She has not yet learned to put herself in other people's shoes and see a situation from their perspective. That is something I can teach her."

Thinking her new thoughts would help Patricia feel calmer, more compassionate, and connected to herself. Her new thoughts would allow her to transition from the fear of being judged and her daughter growing up to be a selfish, disrespectful, and inconsiderate person to a place of love. From that place, Patricia would have been able to make a better decision on how to respond to the situation in order to achieve the desired result. For instance, she could have reminded Madison to watch her manners and eat her cake with a fork. Patricia could have done it in a loving, but firm voice (to convey that she was serious) or in a playful way to give her daughter a chance to change her action without feeling embarrassed in front of the guests. "The birthday girl must have forgotten her manners in the kitchen sink. Let's go wash her hands and bring those manners to the table."

5. **Practice Thinking New Thoughts.** Practicing thinking her new thoughts every time a similar situation

occurs would help Patricia respond more intentionally and create a more connected relationship with Madison.

James:

1. **Become Aware of the Feeling.** Noticing that he did not like his daughter's behavior, James could have used the space to become aware of his feelings. He could have asked, "What am I feeling right now?" to identify his feeling and respond with, "I feel irritated."

2. **Become Aware of Your Thoughts.** Once he connected with the feeling in his body, he could have asked, "What am I thinking right now? What are the thoughts I am having that are creating this feeling?" "My friends think highly of Patricia and me as parents. They think we're doing a great job raising Madison. I think, though, that if they see Madison behaving this way, they'll think that she doesn't know how to behave at the table. They will conclude that we are incapable and not as good as we seem to be. I'm afraid that if I tell my daughter to stop right now, she might not listen to me, and if she doesn't, my friends might see me as a parent who can't manage my child's behavior. If they do, they'll stop respecting me."

3. **Evaluate Your Thoughts.** "Is continuing to think these thoughts going to cause me to respond in the way that will help me connect with Madison?" Evaluating his thoughts would help James realize that continuing to think these thoughts would lead to him feeling even more irritated or embarrassed while avoiding the problem.

4. **Decide What You Want to Think.** Keeping in mind that he had the freedom to choose his thoughts and by doing so change how he feels, he could think instead, "Yes, my daughter's eating cake with her fingers. Yes, I don't like it. But that's ok. It doesn't mean that I am a bad parent. It simply means that, unintentionally, she found a less than ideal way of meeting her need for variety. It's her birthday. I think we can make a one-time exception for now. However, I'll talk to her later tonight and review what we taught her about table manners to make sure that she knows that I did notice her behavior and understands that there are better choices she could make."

Thinking this way would help James connect with himself and stay true to his values while remaining connected with his daughter instead of pretending that he was fine with something that irritated him by blocking his emotions and chasing away his thoughts about Madison's actions. James would feel calm and confident in himself being able to make well-considered parenting choices. His decision to address the issue later instead of ignoring it would allow him to genuinely continue enjoying his conversations with the guests and connect with his daughter by having a one-on-one conversation about her manners in a loving, respectful, and caring way.

5. **Practice Thinking New Thoughts.** Practicing thinking his new thoughts in similar situations would allow James to connect with Madison and feel better as a parent while staying true to his values.

Revealing the Subconscious

Remember, our protective, caring brain makes our thoughts automatic and subconscious because it helps us save energy and be more efficient in getting the desired results. Can you imagine having to think about each step when you are brushing your teeth every morning? "First, I get my toothbrush...Next, I turn on the faucet and get my toothbrush wet. Then..." Even to describe these three steps, I had to make a mental effort and imagine brushing my teeth in the morning.

I recommend you try it and notice: do you remember everything you do when brushing your teeth in exact detail? What you will find is that, although you are proficient in brushing your teeth and do it regularly, you will have to make a mental effort in order to remember every single detail, such as what side you start brushing first and whether you begin with brushing your upper or lower teeth on that side.

Your brain will not like this exercise because it has to spend energy consciously thinking about unconscious actions. If your brain had to think consciously about your every action every morning, such as making a bed, putting your clothes on, driving your car to work, by the time you get to work, you would be exhausted and ready to go home and get in bed. So, your brain does you a favor—it saves you from physical and mental fatigue by making the thoughts you think regularly subconscious. Once they become subconscious, you stop being aware of those thoughts. Because they are so familiar to you, you cling to them like a child to her blanket and leave them running there unquestioned.

Changing the way we think is not something that comes naturally to us. We have practiced our current way of thinking for so long that it became programmed into our brains. Every time we think a thought, the neurons communicate with one another. The more often we think a particular thought, the more often those neurons communicate, forming connections. Eventually, those thoughts become automatic and subconscious. That's how our thoughts become our beliefs.

Our beliefs become part of us and end up guiding our choices. This serves us well in most cases. The problem is that when we make thoughts that are not serving us subconscious, we unintentionally end up creating emotional suffering and unwanted results in our lives.

Patience and Practice

It may seem as if this process of changing your thinking takes a long time. You are probably wondering how you are supposed to change your thinking and feelings when you are under pressure to act in stressful situations?

Firstly, although it may sound like applying the Parenting Success Formula takes a long time, it does not take hours or even minutes to implement. When practiced enough, using the formula only takes seconds. It may take you longer to apply the formula at the beginning because it is a new skill. Your brain is unfamiliar with this process, and, like with any new skill, it requires repetition, awareness, and commitment to deliberate practice.

Think about learning to drive a car. When one begins practicing, everything seems cumbersome and overwhelming. There are so many things to remember to do and not do when driving. Initially, when focusing on the road, one forgets about watching their speed. When focusing on keeping a safe passing distance, one forgets to turn on the turn signal. Eventually, due to neuroplasticity, people learn to drive effortlessly, efficiently, and automatically. Now, in addition to driving the car without deliberately thinking about every single move, people listen to their favorite songs on the radio and sing along while helping children in the backseat resolve their argument. The skill of driving a car seems natural.

The same will happen with your skill of applying the Parenting Success Formula. With enough practice, you will become more efficient and effective at using the Parenting Success Formula, even in unexpected and unfamiliar situations.

Secondly, remember that sometimes it is worth it to take time to take space, even if it is just for a split second, to connect with yourself rather than taking action you might regret later. Using the Parenting Success Formula helps parents realize that they often do not even have to immediately take action. When they connect with themselves, they begin thinking much clearer and see that the situation is not as stressful and urgent as it seemed to be. From a self-connected place, they can make better decisions and see the options they had not considered before. When you take time to connect with yourself, you may be pleasantly surprised by the creative parenting options you come up with.

The Parenting Success Formula has become a life-changing tool for many families, and it can become one for you, too. In order to get the most out of it, you need to build a strong foundation by learning to think new, empowering thoughts and practice thinking those thoughts until they become your beliefs. Discover what your new empowering beliefs might be in the next chapter.

The Parenting Success Formula Action Step

Your *Parenting Connection Workbook* is filled with exercises and questions that lead you through a process similar to what I use with my private coaching clients to transform their parent-child relationships. Visit www.albinspire.com/workbook to download your copy of the workbook.

6

TRANSFORMING YOUR BELIEFS

My grandpa, who had some experience and knew a lot about building structures, explained to me when I was little that an old, weak foundation can compromise the quality and strength of a new house built in the place of an old one.

The same is true about your beliefs and parent-child relationship. If you want to build a new, life-long, fully connected parent-child relationship, you need to start by replacing the old foundation—your old beliefs—with new ones.

A Strong Foundation

Below are fifteen foundational beliefs that can help you create a deep connection with your child. You may notice that some of these beliefs may be easier for you to welcome and adopt, while you may feel resistance against others. It is completely natural because some of these beliefs may contradict your previously held beliefs and require you to step out of your comfort zone to make a change.

Just remind yourself that that is how our brain reacts to

something new. However, if you give these new beliefs a chance, your parent-child relationship will transform. As American author Ross Greene said, "The only prerequisite is an open mind."[1]

Foundational Beliefs

1. There is no good or bad behavior.

"What? How can you say that? What about my child pushing his sister? What about him calling me stupid? What about pulling the cat's tail and laughing?"

Over five hundred years ago, William Shakespeare said, "There is nothing either good or bad, but thinking makes it so." Just like many other things and events in life, behavior is neither good nor bad. It just takes place. It is our judgment, labeling, and thinking about the behavior that makes it good or bad. There is a Russian song, "У природы нет плохой погоды," which translates as "Nature does not have bad weather." A parent who was planning to take the family to the beach in the afternoon is going to think of the rain as an issue, get upset, and call it "bad weather," while a parent who just finished planting flowers with her children is going to think of the rain as a blessing, feel grateful, and consider it good weather.

Similarly, behavior can be thought of differently by different parents, in different cultures, and different circumstances. Take any behavior that you consider bad, and I can guarantee you that there are parents who do not think that behavior is bad. Does your child say he hates you? Some parents would say, "That's ok. He doesn't mean it anyway." Does your child spit and hit? Some parents would say, "That's just kids being kids. What can you do?" Does your child call you stupid? Some parents would say, "You think that's bad? You should hear the names my child calls me!"

Judging, labeling, and forming an opinion about your child's behavior as good or bad is not useful to you or your child. It only distracts you from the real issue. Instead of focusing on formulating an opinion about your child's behavior, focus on looking at the behavior as a fact. Bertrand Russell, the great British philosopher and social critic, was asked on the BBC program *Face-to-Face* in 1959 to share the lessons he had learned in life with future generations. One of the lessons that we need to apply to parenting is the following:

> When you are studying any matter or considering any philosophy, ask yourself only what are the facts and what is the truth that the facts bear out. Never let yourself be diverted either by what you wish to believe or by what you think would have beneficent social effects if it were believed, but look only, and solely at what are the facts.[2]

When Olga adopted the belief that there was no good or bad behavior, she finally became open to genuinely understanding her four-year-old Natasha instead of immediately judging her daughter's behavior. Olga began "studying" Natasha as if she met the child for the first time. By simply objectively observing Natasha's behavior instead of formulating her opinion about her daughter's behavior, Olga stopped seeing her child's "bad" behavior as a deficit but as clues of what kind of skills she still needed to teach her daughter.

In addition to discovering many aspects of her daughter's personality, the mother also gained some peace of mind when liberated from constant "good-or-bad" judgments. Olga stopped getting frustrated about Natasha's behavior and was better able to focus on finding the solution. The belief that there is no good or bad behavior and focusing on the facts will save you from misinterpreting your child's behavior, taking her actions personally, and making parenting mistakes by acting based on the Fight, Freeze, or Flight response.

2. Behavior is a message.

To build a fully connected relationship with your child, recognize that behavior is a message that you need to learn to decode correctly. What do I mean by decoding your child's behavior? Learn to understand what message your child is sending you by behaving in a certain way so that you can choose the most effective, supportive, and appropriate response.

If you do not know how to decode your child's behavior, you might choose to respond in a way that is, although well-intended, not appropriate for addressing the issue your child is struggling with. As a result, instead of connecting, you may end up distancing from one another.

Misdecoding, misinterpreting a child's behavior, is one of the most common mistakes parents make. When a child doesn't listen, parents often see it as a child challenging their authority by being defiant, disrespectful, or manipulative. Fearing "losing control" over the situation, parents often end up yelling at, threatening, or manipulating the child.

There are two parts of this belief that you need to consider. The first is that behavior is one of the main ways a child communicates. Every time your child behaves or misbehaves, he is sending you a message. Our goal is to read the message correctly, just like we would an email. If we do not make a conscious effort to pay close attention to and understand the email we receive, we may misinterpret it and respond differently than if we read it correctly. Our misinterpretation may lead to misunderstanding, confusion, or conflict. The same applies to misinterpreting a child's behavior—a misinterpretation may result in unnecessary emotional suffering.

The second part of this belief is that two kinds of messages are sent through behavior. One is an "I feel good" message, and the other one is an "I need help!" message. American author, spiritual leader, politician, and activist Marianne Williamson put it really well when she said, "Everything we do is either an act of love or a cry for help."

On the one hand, when your child listens to you, hugs you, or kisses you, he sends you a message that he's doing alright emotionally. He feels safe, loved, and connected to you and himself.

On the other hand, when your child displays challenging behavior, he sends you a message that he needs help, which may help with connecting with himself, finding constructive ways to meet his needs, or learning a new skill.

The child with challenging behavior is not trying to give you a hard time. He is signaling to you that *he* is having a hard time. The only reason he uses this type of behavior to express his needs and feelings to you is that he has not yet learned how to express them in a better way by first connecting with himself to process his feelings properly.

When, for instance, a child gets upset, "Why does Viktoria's mom buy her new toys every time they go to the store, and you don't?" or "You gave Leilani more sparkly stickers. It's not fair," it may sound like he is being greedy, envious, or difficult, but the true message that he's sending you is, "I feel like you love me less than Viktoria's mother loves her," or "I feel like I'm less worthy than Leilani."

Even though it may not come across that way, that is what the child truly feels. It does not mean that you have to begin buying toys for him every time you go to the store or give him the same number of stickers to convince him that he is good enough and that you love him. You still need to stay true to yourself and do what's best for both of you. The only difference is that you will use the information you learn from his messages to better understand and help him find constructive ways to meet his needs.

Believing that behavior is a message will help you see your child's behavior as a way of communicating with you. You can then use his message to decide how to respond in a way that allows him to feel heard and brings you closer to one another.

3. There is positive intent behind a child's behavior.

"Do you mean to say that when my child hits his brother with a toy instead of sharing, he has positive intent? He obviously understands that he's hurting his brother!" Although it may seem that a child's intent is to hurt another, destroy things, or harm himself, it is not his real intent. The child's ultimate intent is to take care of his needs.

Why does the brain cause the child to use destructive ways to do so? It either does not yet know a better way to handle it or has not internalized it yet to overcome its emotional biological response under stress and needs more practice with guidance and support from you.

4. The child is not his behavior.

A harmful mistake that many parents make is equating the child with his behavior. They think that if the child's behavior is "bad," it means that the child is "bad." They believe that when they don't approve of the child's behavior, they have to not approve of the child either. Therefore, they often criticize or shame the child as a person, hoping to change his behavior. "Look at your room! It looks like a pigsty. Why are you so lazy?"

While well-intended, such comments may lead to the child's low self-esteem and poor self-image. Because the child bases his opinion of himself on others' opinions and feedback, especially by the authority figures in his life, and because he has not yet developed the ability to evaluate others' opinions and feedback critically, he accepts them as facts.

Remembering that the child's lovability and worthiness are unquestionable and separating the child from his behavior will help you focus on the child's actions. Doing so keeps your child's self-esteem untarnished and allows you to connect with your child and help him make better choices.

Instead of criticizing your child in order to get him to clean up his room, you can choose to talk to him to find out why he doesn't clean up. Is it because he does not think it's important? Is it because he is too tired to do it right after school? Is it because he has learned that you will do it for him if he doesn't clean up? When you know the reason behind your child's behavior, you will be able to teach him what he needs to know in a loving and supporting way and help him come up with an optimal solution. Instead of feeling criticized and judged, the child will feel cared for, supported, and more open to changing his behavior.

5. Any behavior can be changed.

What parents often fear the most is that if the child has a habitual way of behaving, there is little or nothing that can be done to help the child change his behavior. Nothing can be further from the truth. The fact that all behavior is learned and can be unlearned was proven by the research conducted by behaviorists in the early 1900.[3] With the discoveries in neuroscience, we now know that behavioral changes can be made consciously and purposefully. We also know that the brain displays the greatest plasticity in childhood, which allows a child to learn a new way of behaving faster than an adult.

One of the main reasons why many parents' efforts are not effective in helping their children learn to behave differently is they use providing the information and repetition as a way to support the child in changing his behavior. How often have you heard from a parent, "How many times do I have to tell you…"? The truth is that by only repeating what you want to teach your child, you are more likely to annoy your child and create resistance rather than get him interested in cooperating. Learning a new behavior is the same as learning a new skill. As Joe Dispenza explains in his book *Evolve Your Brain*:

> Whether we physically or mentally acquire a skill, there are four elements that we all use to change our brains: learning knowledge, receiving hands-on instruction, paying attention, and repetition.
>
> Learning is making synaptic connections; instruction gets the body involved in order to have a new experience, which further enriches the brain. When we also pay attention and repeat our new skill over and over again, our brains will change.[4]

That is why I teach my clients that they need to get all the elements involved. For example, telling your child, "Don't talk to your sister like that!" while he's in the middle of an argument with his sister is most likely not going to work. Why? Because for your child to successfully implement the behavior you want to teach him, he needs to at least pay attention to what you are teaching.

Having hands-on experience by practicing what the child needs to say considerably increases his chances of behaving in this new way. So, if he says, "Shut up!" to his sister when she's trying to talk to him when he's watching his favorite TV show, you could teach him to say, "Could you please wait until I'm done watching the show to talk to me?" Finally, he may need to practice with you a few times to internalize his new behavior through repetition.

6. Conflict is an opportunity to connect.

Because parents crave love and connection, they do not like—and often avoid—conflicts because they see conflicts as negative experiences that only distances them from their children. The truth is that *their beliefs* about conflicts are what really distances them. If parents believe that conflicts are harmful and weaken the connection between them and the child, that will happen. We look for evidence of what we believe and often prove it with our actions. Choosing to believe that conflict is an opportunity to connect will help you feel more open to learning more about your child's fears, needs, and thoughts and connect with him through offering your understanding, compassion, and presence even during conflicts.

When Margaret believed that conflict had to be a negative experience, in which only one can be a winner, she came from a place of fear. When her eight-year-old son Gerhard refused to do his math homework, she immediately moved into fight mode and threatened to take away Gerhard's video game time. Gerhard would get angry, argue with Margaret, and accuse her of being mean. That was a common scenario. Exhausted from constant arguments and feeling disconnected, the mother and son dreaded homework time.

When Margaret adopted her new belief that conflict is an opportunity to connect, she shared with him how much she disliked arguing with him and asked if there was anything she could do to support him. Gerhard began crying. It turned out that Gerhard avoided doing his homework because it was too hard for him. It was challenging for him to keep up with the school math curriculum, so he fell behind. Being able to share his true feelings with Margaret allowed Gerhard to feel closer to her and allowed Margaret to be compassionate toward Gerhard. She effectively supported her son with his academic progress and confidence by being there for him and hiring a tutor for him.

7. My feelings and actions are my responsibility.

Often, parents blame their child for "making" them feel or act a certain way. "I didn't want to be mean, but I had to because she really pushed my buttons," "She makes me feel guilty when she says that I don't love her," "He drives me crazy!"

When you think that your child is responsible for how you feel or what you do, you keep him accountable for your feelings and actions. Your inner state and behavior are now utterly dependent on how he chooses to behave. It means that your child has to change what he says or does in order for you to feel and behave differently. Believing that your feelings and actions depend on your child's behavior will cause you to attempt to control your child in order for you to feel and act better, which is unfair to you and your child.

Since childhood, we have been taught to look for something or someone outside of ourselves to blame when something is not going our way. What does a toddler hear from a caring and comforting parent when he bumps his head into a table? "Poor thing! You've got a boo-boo? Did the table hit you on the head? Bad table!" This puts all the blame on the table and does not teach the child to take responsibility for his actions, accept and deal with the consequences, and learn from his mistakes. What about asking your upset child, "Did Bobby make you angry? That's not nice!" By blaming the other child, the parent teaches the child that the other is responsible for his feelings, and there is not much that the child can do to change his feelings, which leaves the child feeling helpless and resentful.

We also learned that we could get out of trouble by simply pointing the finger at something or someone else, "That's not my fault. He pushed me first!" or my students' favorite, "I didn't want to, but she made me!"

The problem with that is blaming others for how we feel results in developing a victim mentality. We feel like things are being done *to* us. When we feel like things are being done *to* us, we believe that we cannot do anything about it and, thus, don't even try to do anything to change the situation or solve the problem. It doesn't need to be this way. To prevent having a victim mentality, become vigilant about the language you use. Decide to stop using "I have to" and "It/she/he made me," and begin using "I get to" and "I choose to."

For example, instead of thinking or saying, "I *have to* take my daughter to soccer practice," use, "I *get to* take my daughter to soccer practice." Instead of "My daughter *made me* so mad when she threw her jacket on the floor again instead of putting it into the closet!" use "I *chose to get* mad when she throws her jacket on the floor again instead of putting it into the closet." The truth is that you are the one who gets to choose how you feel and respond to everything that happens in your parent-child relationship. Your child cannot "make" you feel anything, even if he gives you a reason to feel unpleasant emotions.

When you change the language you use, you will be more capable of changing your feelings, actions, and results. You will stop seeing yourself as a victim and your child as a villain. Regardless of how your child chooses to behave, you will remain the one who gets to decide how you are going to respond.

8. I am not responsible for my child's feelings.

When I ask parents what they want the most from life, unanimously, they tell me they want their child to be happy. Many parents see making their child happy as their biggest daily responsibility and life purpose. They do not realize that by doing so, they put tremendous pressure on themselves and the child.

On the one hand, parents who make their child's feelings of happiness their responsibility usually end up constantly worrying about how to adjust the world in ways that they believe will make their child happy. When parents do their best but see that their child still experiences unhappiness, they may feel disappointed in themselves and feel guilty about not being "good enough" or capable of making their child happy. Some parents may even resent the child for not feeling happy after all they have done for the child, and despite the sacrifices they have made.

On the other hand, seeing how much their parents do to make sure they always feel happy, some children may feel guilty when they feel unhappy because it causes them to seem ungrateful. They may beat themselves up for not being happy, despite their parents' efforts to ensure that they are always happy.

Other children get used to parents pleasing them and making their every wish come true to ensure their happiness, so they often begin taking their parents' generosity for granted and expect parents to do even more for them. When children get used to their happiness being their parents' responsibility, they grow up to be unhappy adults waiting for others to "make" them happy, blame others for their unhappiness, and complain about life being unfair whenever they don't get what they want. They often end up feeling victimized, giving up quickly, and blaming parents for not being good enough or not giving them enough—enough opportunities, love, money, or knowledge.

In either case, taking responsibility for your child's happiness neither works nor helps you or your child. You can't "make" your child feel a certain way. You may spend all your life trying to create and rearrange the circumstances in your child's life to protect him from experiencing certain emotions.

Still, it is ultimately his responsibility to create his own happiness by choosing what to think, how to feel, and how to act in those circumstances. The best thing you can do for your child is to teach him how to process their emotions (which you will learn more about in Chapter 8) and use the Parenting Success Formula to create the feelings they want.

9. There are no negative or positive emotions.

Just like there is no good or bad behavior, and no good or bad child, there are no positive or negative emotions. While some may feel more pleasant than others, all emotions are equally important and serve us as signals that allow our body and mind to communicate. Pleasant emotions usually signal that our needs are being met and that we live in accordance with our life principles and values. In contrast, unpleasant emotions let us know that there is something we need to become aware of and possibly change. Unpleasant emotions are like the "Low Fuel" light in a car that lets the driver know the vehicle needs attention. Without it, the driver may not notice that the fuel level was low and continue driving, causing a potential danger for themselves and others on the road.

Because we usually become aware of an emotion before we become aware of the thought that caused it, we need to pay close attention to any emotion we experience. Paying attention to their own emotions and teaching their child to pay attention to his emotions gives parents and the child a chance to take a closer look, reevaluate, and change their thinking if needed in order to be able to replace the emotion with a different one that will help them take a better action.

10. Emotions are meant to be felt.

When parents see their child experiencing what is commonly considered negative emotions, they immediately feel like they have to do something to stop their child from feeling those emotions. They try to "fix" the circumstances, talk the child out of, or distract the child from feeling unpleasant emotions. What they don't realize is that negative emotions don't just go away. In fact, bottling up emotions only causes them to grow more intense. It's like holding your breath. The longer you force yourself to hold your breath, the more intense your body and the need to exhale will become. Eventually, you will need to exhale. It's the same with emotions. Your body reaches its capacity to hold in all those unprocessed emotions. You *will* eventually exhale, and those emotions *will* need to be dealt with.

What is the solution then? In Fred Rogers' words from his book *The World According to Mister Rogers*, "People have said, 'Don't cry' to other people for years and years, and all it has ever meant is, 'I'm too uncomfortable when you show your feelings. Don't cry.' I'd rather have them say, 'Go ahead and cry. I'm here to be with you.'"[5] That's the solution—to learn to allow and experience the emotional discomfort you feel when your child is experiencing unpleasant emotions and teaching your child to process his emotions by allowing them to be there and staying present with his emotions without acting on them.

11. I cannot control my child.

This one will be a tough pill to swallow but hold off your objections and remember to keep an open mind because this is one of the most empowering beliefs that you can have as a parent.

Conventional wisdom teaches us that to be a "good" parent, you must be in control. This is what many parents have learned and what I used to believe. My belief changed when I started a new job where one of my responsibilities was to be in charge of over one hundred students during lunchtime at an elementary school in the cafeteria. Trying to control a number of noisy, crying, screaming, hungry, and arguing children, I would end up feeling like a hopeless and exhausted failure at the end of the day.

After days of running around like a chicken with its head cut off, putting out fire by fire, attempting to get children to behave the "right" way, and feeling as if things were getting out of control, I finally realized that I was simply deceiving myself by believing that I had any control over those children's behaviors. I realized that to make the situation better, I had to let go of my delusion of control.

When hearing the suggestion that they cannot control their child, some parents gasp in disbelief, "What? Are you saying that I have to allow my child to do whatever they want?" No, that's not what I'm saying.

Our society has created the illusion that being a good parent means getting the children to listen to us by behaving the way *we* want them to behave and saying what *we* think is the "right" thing. After many years of practice and working with families, I see two kinds of results when parents attempt to control their children.

One outcome is that parents might end up raising Yes-men and women—obedient wives and husbands, compliant employees, and yielding friends who live their lives trying to satisfy other people's needs, demands, and wishes, and unquestionably adopting others' points of views while being afraid of expressing theirs. These children put their actual needs, values, and wants on the back burner or do not even realize what they are because they never had a chance to look inside themselves and learn what is important to them and what helps them feel fulfilled. They just follow others and trust that someday someone will make them happy.

Alternatively, another outcome is that parents raise children who, craving the freedom of being able to make their own decisions, rebel and choose the opposite from their parents' beliefs, values, and opinions, even if those beliefs, values, and opinions might decrease their quality of life. Wanting to escape their parents' attempts to control them, these children distance themselves from their parents, often both emotionally and physically.

If you cannot control your child, what can you do to help them make the choices that will serve them? Inspire! You can inspire your child to make wise choices, respect you, and want to feel connected to you by giving him the freedom of choice, listening to him and acknowledging his voice, respecting him, recognizing and appreciating his uniqueness, and believing in him. You can inspire him by being a role model, being an example of the kind of person you want your child to be when he grows up while also allowing him to stay true to himself and decide who he wants to be. You can teach your child, show him the options he does not yet see, and allow him to determine if any of them work for him or support him in finding his own.

With my students in the cafeteria, I told them that I had decided that it was everyone's responsibility—not just mine—to keep the cafeteria clean and quiet enough for everyone to be able to enjoy eating and conversing with their friends. We discussed and agreed upon our rules. I explained that we would keep each other accountable by kindly reminding those who forget our rules and helping each other clean up.

To make it fun and recognize those children who were being responsible, we would select a table team that did the best job following our rules each day. That table would get a point. At the end of the week, we would calculate points to see which table performed consistently well during the week and celebrate them. We also agreed that the tables that did not win would not get discouraged but cheer for and get inspired by the one who won and would do their best the following week.

The students loved it! First, they grew closer as a team. They were excited and proud to see their tables clean and were kind and attentive to their teammates as they helped one another clean the spots they missed. To help the students feel even more special, I would take a picture of the table team that won and put it up on the "Table Team of the Week" poster I had on the wall. I also suggested that they pick a name for their table. Being able to choose a name for themselves and have ownership of their accomplishments enabled them to feel even more significant and connected as teammates.

Soon, the atmosphere in the cafeteria, as well as the students themselves, changed. Teams began supporting each other! When students noticed that one of the tables had not been on the poster for a while, they would encourage those students, root for them, and even help them clean up so they would also get to experience that sense of accomplishment, pride, and team spirit from taking first place.

The students became more excited and began treating each other with compassion and respect. They also felt more respected by me because I trusted and encouraged them now instead of constantly telling them what to do. I would just give them time reminders: how much time they had left to eat, when it was time to start cleaning up, and when to line up to get ready to be dismissed. They had to decide by themselves whether they wanted to participate or not. Nobody was forcing anyone to do anything, but everyone was inspiring and encouraging each other.

You cannot control your child, but you *can* inspire him to behave differently.

12. I'm not superior to my child.

As adults, we often think that we have the right and the responsibility to tell children what to do because we are more intelligent than children. Many parents especially reinforce this belief when they learn about the child's brain development. Some of these parents conclude that they have to "become their child's brain" and do all of the thinking, planning, and reasoning for the child. Avoid making this mistake. Holding this belief may cause you to fall into the trap of feeling superior to the child, which leads to a weaker connection.

What I discovered during my teaching career is that children are much more capable than we often think. My students would frequently develop such creative and intelligent ideas and solutions that we, adults, don't even consider. I also realized that comparing my intelligence to my students' current intelligence and thinking that I was cleverer wasn't fair. All that me being more knowledgeable meant was that I had lived longer on Earth and had more time and opportunities to gain knowledge.

I began wondering, "What if I compared my current skills, abilities, and knowledge to those of my students when they reach my age? Who would actually be smarter?" Considering how quickly technology is developing, how much more interested and savvy younger generations are about exploring it, and how many more ways and opportunities to learn they have nowadays, I wouldn't be surprised if they turn out to be much more intelligent than me. Thinking from this perspective allowed me to appreciate and give children more credit than I would if I was thinking of them as little humans who are less intelligent, incapable of thinking for themselves, and in need of my constant directions.

13. A child is to be as respected as an adult.

Back in the day when I was a nanny, I arrived at the home of the family I worked for. The father looked irritated as he opened the door. "She was supposed to give me her tablet back about half an hour ago," he pointed at five-year-old Rita hiding under the table as soon as we entered the living room.

"I have been chasing her ever since. The baby is taking a nap upstairs. I gotta take off now. Take it away from her," said the father as he looked in the direction of the table again.

As soon as the door behind the father closed, I kneeled next to the table to see Rita. She heard what her father said, so when she saw me kneel, she pressed her tablet against her chest as if her life depended on it and screamed at the top of her lungs, "It's mine! It's mine! It's mine! And you won't take it away from me!" She gave me a fierce look as if she was ready to continue the fight that she had started with her father, if I attempted to take what belonged to her—her precious tablet.

At that moment, all I saw was a little, scared child who needed a small slice of security. Her parents were traveling a lot, and she never felt like she could keep them close to her. She could not keep her friendships either because her family moved frequently. They just moved to a new town. Not only did she feel insecure about what was going to happen next, what else was going to be taken away from her, but she was feeling like her voice did not matter, "Who cares what I want? Adults are going to make all the decisions anyway."

I imagined if it were an adult in front of me. Would I take away her computer just because her time was up? No, I know that it would be disrespectful, and I would feel uncomfortable. But how is this situation different? Just because the child is physically smaller than me, do I have the right to force her to give me her tablet?

Considering the above questions and seeing how much it mattered to her to keep the tablet, I said, "I'm not going to take it away from you, Rita." Her facial expression softened with a surprised but still suspicious look. "I want to have it," she said, still not quite believing what I just said. "I understand, and I respect that. I agree—the tablet belongs to you, and you have the right to have it." Her body seemed to relax with relief because she did not have to fight anymore.

"I'm going to go check on the baby," I said. "I will be back." Rita waited for me to walk away at a safe enough distance to relieve her grip on the tablet and started entering the password to unlock it. When I came back, she was watching a cartoon. I sat on the floor far from the table so that she would not assume that I came to take the tablet away.

"I'm going to build a block tower," I said to Rita. "You're welcome to join me whenever you want to." She did not look up and continued demonstratively staring at the screen to show me that she clearly preferred watching the cartoon rather than playing with me. I was only on my third block when I noticed with the corner of my eye that she was quietly crawling out from under the table toward me. She stood up when she approached me, "Can I join you?" Rita asked. I knew that she was going to join me soon. The reason she wanted the tablet was not as much for the sake of the tablet itself, but just to make sure that she had some security in her new home. She wanted to feel respected; she wanted to feel heard.

Genuinely respecting the children I work with as much as I would adults has always helped me understand them better and feel compassionate toward them. We are all human. We all want to know that we matter. Believing that a child is to be as respected as an adult will help you feel compassionate and help them feel understood and respected.

14. Those who love and care about me will not judge me for being who I am.

One of my favorite Dr. Seuss's quotes is, "Be who you are and say what you mean because those who mind don't matter and those who matter don't mind."

As I talked to Nadine during a home visit, her three-year-old son Asad kept pulling on her sweater's sleeve. Nadine continued talking to me, acting as if nothing was happening.

When it was my turn to talk, I paused and asked her with genuine curiosity, "Are you OK with Asad pulling on your sleeve?"

Nadine seemed slightly embarrassed. "No, not really," she replied.

"Why don't you ask him to stop?"

Nadine shared with me that she often tolerated his behavior that she did not like because she was afraid that if she told Asad to stop it and he did not listen, she would not know what to do. She couldn't bear the thought of others judging her. I told Nadine what I wish I had been told a while ago when I started working with children: be who you are and stay true to your values, regardless of what others think of you, because Dr. Suess was right—those who care about you will not judge you. Instead, they will empathize with you, hear you out, and offer their support.

On the other hand, the opinions of those who choose to judge you don't need to bother you. Others judging you does not mean that there is something wrong with you or that they are bad people. They simply do not know you, your child, or your situation well enough to understand you. In most cases, it is not even about you.

What's important is for you not to try to please everyone and get them to like you, but rather be who you are and act on what truly matters to you. Permit others to judge you, even if it causes you emotional discomfort. This will give you an opportunity to practice thinking purposefully in order to feel comfortable with emotional discomfort, depend less on the opinions of others, and stay connected to yourself.

15. Judging and criticizing myself is not going to help me connect with my child.

Self-judgement, self-criticism, and self-loathing are very common among parents. The restless inner voice in their

93

heads is constantly following them day and night, lecturing about how they should be different, telling them what they should and should not be doing, and judging them for what they have or have not done.

They believe that looking at themselves through a microscope to find every single thing they do that is "wrong" and pointing it out in a self-deprecating way is somehow supposed to encourage or inspire them to be or do better in their relationship with their child.

If that worked, why would so many parents feel like they were not good enough? The answer is, in the words of Geneen Roth, the author of *Feeding the Hungry Heart*, "We don't change from force, from deprivation, from guilt, and from punishment. We don't change because we back ourselves into a wall and say, 'Change or else!'"[6] True change occurs when it is made from the place of love, self-connection, and self-care.

When coaching, I often ask my clients, "How does talking to yourself in a self-deprecating way feel?" Inevitably, most of them respond that it feels like they are unlovable and unworthy. When you feel unlovable and unworthy, what are the chances that you will be able to, or even want to, connect with yourself? Little to none. Being disconnected from yourself and judging yourself will prevent you from connecting with your child because when you judge yourself, you also judge your child. And, as Mother Teresa said, "If you judge people, you have no time to love them." If you don't have time to love them, you don't feel connected to them.

Learn to quiet that self-deprecating voice in your head and develop a loving and compassionate voice. By being appreciative of and kind to yourself, you will also be giving your child a role model for how they need to treat themselves and others.

Empowering Yourself with New Beliefs

Changing your beliefs may feel challenging because it is in our nature to resist the unfamiliar, and change is unfamiliar. Know that there is nothing wrong with you if you are struggling to embrace some of these beliefs right now. Instead of beating yourself up for finding it difficult to accept these new beliefs or arguing against them, begin with putting into practice those beliefs that are easier for you to accept. Give yourself time and permission to love yourself throughout your parenting journey no matter what, knowing that these new beliefs are always available to you and will empower you as a parent.

Adopting these transformational beliefs about yourself and your child will lay the solid foundation you need to build the fully connected parent-child relationship you have always wanted. Another factor required for this foundation to last is your ability to stay self-connected. This is an ability that you can strengthen by practicing. In the next chapter, you will find twenty effective ways to practice staying self-connected.

Transforming Your Beliefs
Action Step

Continue to make progress toward creating the connected parent-child relationship you and your child deserve by completing the exercises in your *Parenting Connection Workbook* to discover how your beliefs have been impacting your parenting and how you might incorporate new foundational beliefs into your life and parenting. If you haven't already, you can download the workbook at www.albinspire.com/workbook.

PART III

EMPOWERING YOURSELF AND YOUR CHILD WITH EMOTIONAL MASTERY

7

STAYING SELF-CONNECTED

There are moments in every parent's life when, in response to their child's behavior, they forget everything their brilliant thinking brain knows and believes and unintentionally let their primal brain take charge. This causes them to take actions that they regret and beat themselves up about later.

Being too hard on yourself isn't healthy or helpful to either you or your child. You are human. You are learning, and you are going to make mistakes. Parenting is not about being perfect and doing everything "right." It's about learning from your mistakes and practicing staying self-connected so that you can prevent making the same mistakes in the future.

Your Three Powers

I have devoted this chapter to sharing practical ways to help you stay connected with yourself and remember what's important to you, even when dealing with challenging parenting situations. These ways are based on the human brain's unique abilities, such as remembering, imagining, and asking questions.

The power of memory is to be able to retrieve the information you need from your brain whenever you need it. The power of imagination is that you do not have to wait for things to happen for you to figure out how to handle them. You can prepare yourself by visualizing situations in your mind and making choices that you believe are best for you and your child in advance. The power of asking questions is that our brain is wired to answer questions. It gets stimulated by curiosity. When you pose a question, it triggers a mental reflex known as "instinctive elaboration."[1] Your brain mobilizes all its energy looking for the answer to that question. The quality of the questions you ask will determine the quality of the results you get. For example, you would get a different result if you asked, "What's wrong with my child?" than if you asked, "How can I help my child?"

Using all three powers—the power of your imagination, memory, and questioning—will help you connect with yourself by bringing to the forefront of your mind what really matters to you. Then, from that connected, peaceful, and loving state, you can connect with your child to help them feel connected, peaceful, and loving as well.

Twenty Ways to Stay Self-Connected

1. Say what you need to hear. Ask yourself, "What do I need to hear right now to feel____?" Our society has taught us to rely on other people to acknowledge our uniqueness, worthiness, and effort in order to feel good about ourselves. The truth is that you can create the feeling you want to have about yourself by telling yourself what you want to hear from others.

For instance, when you feel overwhelmed with your child's behavior and have no idea what to do, instead of thinking that you are an incompetent parent, ask yourself,

"What do I need to hear right now in order to feel that I'm a competent parent?" Your answer could be, "The fact that I don't know what to do right now has nothing to do with who I am as a parent. All it means is that I do not have the answer right now, and it's ok. I will find the answer. For now, I'll just do the best I can with the resources I have."

2. Take space. In stressful situations, our primary brain panics and demands we react to the situation right away by making it feel dangerous and urgent. When you are feeling stressed, overwhelmed, or uncertain, don't rush to take action. Instead, remind yourself of Viktor Frankl's quote, "Between stimulus and response there is a space. In that space is our power to choose our response. In our response lies our growth and our freedom,"[2] and ask yourself:

- Do I really have to respond right now to what is happening?
- Am I taking space to connect with myself?
- Am I using this space to have thoughts that calm me down or thoughts that cause me to feel even more anxious?
- What would happen if I responded later when I feel connected with myself?

You can also tell yourself, "I don't have to act right now. I can wait a few seconds (minutes, or sometimes even days when it's appropriate) to make a decision and prepare myself to respond in a way that will help my child learn what I want to teach her."

3. Response/react check. Ask yourself, "Am I responding or reacting right now?" If you find yourself in Fight, Flight, or Freeze modes, that is how you know that you are reacting and need to pause and take the "space"

Viktor Frankl talked about in order to connect with yourself first and respond consciously.

4. Correctly decode the message. When you are feeling angry, frustrated, or disappointed with your child's behavior, remember Marianne Williamson's quote, "Everything we do is either an act of love or a cry for help." Ask yourself, "What message is my child sending me?" Asking this question will help you remember that your child's challenging behavior is her way of asking you for help. You will notice yourself feeling compassionate instead of irritated or frustrated with her behavior.

Then, proceed with asking yourself, "How can I help my child?" or "What does my child need help with right now?" These questions will help you focus on what is really important—helping her find better ways of dealing with whatever she needs help with, whether it's constructively handling her emotions or tying her shoes.

5. Stop taking your child's behavior personally. Parents often react instead of responding to a situation because they take things personally. For example, if the child does not listen to the parent, the parent may interpret it as the child being disrespectful. Instead of taking things personally, remind yourself that your child's behavior is not about you. It's about her brain's interpretation of the situation and reaction to it.

When feeling stressed, scared, or angry, the child's primal brain prevails over her thinking brain and puts her in F3 mode. When she is in F3 mode, you are the last person whose thoughts and feelings she is thinking about. This is not because she doesn't love or care about you, but because she's focused on her own needs at that moment.

Instead of getting angry, upset, or disappointed with

your child's behavior, remember what you learned about the six human needs and ask yourself:

- What need is my child attempting to meet?
- How can I help her meet that need in a different, constructive (kind, loving, caring) way?

6. Let go of control. When you feel tension and resistance in your parent-child relationship, it is often a sign that, unwittingly, you may be attempting to control your child or the situation. Because your brain likes familiarity and predictability, it causes you to feel scared when something doesn't go the way you planned. To regain the feeling of safety and comfort, you try to take control. The problem is that our attempts to control situations or the child are caused by fear, which makes it impossible to connect.

To get yourself out of a place of fear and increase awareness so that you can move yourself into a loving, connected place, ask yourself, "Am I trying to control my child?" or "Am I trying to control the situation in order to meet my need for certainty?" If you are completely honest with yourself, you will admit that there are things out of your control, and your child's behavior is one of them.

Your answer will remind you that the belief that you can control your child is just an illusion and will help you begin to look for productive ways of meeting your need for certainty. You may meet that need by connecting with and inspiring your child to change her behavior through explicit teaching, firm belief in your child's ability to make better behavior choices, and encouragement.

7. Don't make assumptions. One of the four agreements that Don Miguel Ruiz writes about in his book

The Four Agreements: A Practical Guide to Personal Freedom is "Don't make assumptions."[3] Have you ever been so certain that something was true that you were ready to bet on it, only to find out later that you were mistaken? Maybe you've scolded your child for losing her hat, only to find out later that you accidentally left it in the dryer? Perhaps you've been certain she didn't complete her homework, only to be proven wrong when she showed you all of her finished work.

The human brain is really good at making assumptions based on our beliefs and past experiences. For example, if your child has lied to you a few times in the past, next time she is telling you the truth, you will be less likely to believe her. By making assumptions, our brain creates decision-making shortcuts. It tries to save us energy by protecting us from all the analysis a new situation requires.

However, the problem with making assumptions is that it prevents us from considering the uniqueness of a new situation and looking for the most appropriate way to deal with it. Using an approach that worked in the past may not be applicable to the new situation and lead to weakening your connection with your child.

Learn to recognize and stop making assumptions by asking yourself the following questions:

- Am I making assumptions about my child right now?
- Am I looking at the situation with fresh eyes?
- Do I have enough information to form my opinion?
- Is it true, or do I *assume* it's true?
- Is it a fact or my opinion?
- What are the facts?

Doing your best to figure out what is factual instead of making assumptions will help you stay objective and avoid making mistakes.

8. Be proactive—have a plan. Imagine you and your child are going to a party. You know that you will stay there past your child's bedtime. As most parents would, you hope that she will not have a meltdown. The problem with that is when you *hope* that it's not going to happen, you don't really know what to expect because it might or might not happen. You may feel uncertain, doubtful, and insecure. When you are unprepared, you are more likely to act from a place of fear.

The question is, why rely on hope when it is in your power to feel certain and confident that you can affect the outcome and successfully handle whatever happens by preparing for it? If you have the slightest concern that something you do not want to happen may happen, plan on it happening. When you plan on something happening, you can create a plan for how to prevent it from happening or how to handle it constructively if it does happen.

If you know that the child might have a meltdown because she will get tired staying up past her bedtime at the party, plan on her having a meltdown. Come up with a plan by spending some time thinking about what you can do to either prevent a meltdown or help your child get through the meltdown. When you plan ahead, you have the luxury of time to make decisions with your thinking brain while in a calm and connected state. What's the worst thing that can happen if you are prepared for an undesirable situation that does not happen? You have a great time while feeling relaxed and confident, and you'll have a plan for the next time.

9. Become curious. When you notice your blood pressure rising, heartbeat accelerating, and less than kind words are about to burst out of your mouth, it can often be a sign that you are judging and condemning your child's behavior. Use this as an indication that you need to shift your thinking. Instead of judging and condemning, begin observing your child with genuine curiosity because, as Gay Hendricks writes in his book, *The Big Leap*, "You can learn a lot more with a spirit of wonder and enjoyment than you can with an attitude of criticism."[4]

One of the biggest mistakes parents make is believing that they know their child 100%. The truth is that you don't know your child completely. Just because you know that your child's favorite color has been green does not mean it's still his favorite color. People change. They change their opinions, preferences, and perspectives. It is our nature to change. Our brains change slightly every single time we think a thought or learn something new. When our brains change, the complexity, quality, and context of our thinking change as well. As you know from the Parenting Success Formula, our emotions and actions also change when our thinking changes. Because children are learning a massive amount of new information daily, their brains are changing at an even greater speed.

If your child was playing with an older child whom she looks up to earlier today, and the child mentioned that her favorite color was yellow, your child may decide her favorite color is now yellow as well. You may not even know about it until the next day when she refuses to drink juice out of her favorite green cup and insists on you pouring her juice into a yellow cup, which you do not even have.

Instead of using your past experiences with your child and being sure that you know your child 100%, use moments when she changes her mind or shows a side of her you haven't seen before to get to know that side of your child. Imagine meeting her for the first time. Pay close attention to what she is doing and how, learn why she is doing it, and notice patterns. Study her behavior as if you were a scientist.

To help you in your never-ending child discovery quest, you may choose to use the following "I wonder..." statements and ask yourself the "How" questions:

- I wonder what my child is thinking right now.
- I wonder what my child is feeling right now.
- I wonder what caused my child to behave this way.
- How might my child be seeing me at this moment?
- How might my child be feeling around me right now?
- How might my child be interpreting my behavior right now?

If appropriate, have a discussion with the child to determine if the answers you thought of match what the child is really feeling and thinking.

Never stop studying your child. Genuinely do your best to understand your child's perspective by becoming curious, and you will be amazed at how much you can learn about your child and how much closer you two will become.

10. Put yourself in your child's shoes. I am sure you have heard this before. Maybe you have even tried putting yourself in your child's shoes, but, for some reason, it just didn't work out for you. Here is why it most likely didn't. When parents attempt to imagine themselves in their child's situation in order to understand or empathize with their child, they do it by remembering themselves as a child and thinking from that perspective.

Sometimes that strategy works, but it often doesn't because, although the parents manage to imagine themselves in the child's situation, their perspective is based on their own childhood experiences. I recommend entirely forgetting about your own experiences and how you would feel. Focus on your child's current and past experiences and what she is doing and saying right now. I encourage you to think about what you have said or done before your child's behavior escalated, maybe consider what happened in your child's life earlier that day, week, month, or even year, and then ask yourself the following questions:

- If I were my child, how would I feel about what I, as her parent, just did or said?
- If I were my child, how would I feel about this situation?
- If I were in my child's shoes, what would I like to hear from myself as a parent?
- If I were in my child's situation, what would I not like to hear from myself as a parent right now?

Imagine seeing yourself through your child's eyes at that moment, hearing what you just said, and ask yourself:

- If I heard someone I care about say this to me, what would I be feeling right now?
- Is that how I would like to be treated by an adult with whom I am looking for an emotional connection?

11. "Video camera" effect. This one is a really fun and effective way for you to become aware of your choices when in a stressful situation. Imagine that your interaction with your child is being videotaped on a camera, and there are people on the other side, watching you. I want you to imagine that the people watching are people you respect and who think highly of you as a person and parent. Using this strategy will help you remember your values, become more aware of the actions and choices you make when responding to a situation, and make better decisions at the moment.

12. Replace yourself in your mind. It is fascinating how often we use double standards without even realizing it. Parents often treat their children the way they would never allow other people to treat them.

Sometimes, parents may not like how they are treating their child but, having no idea what else to do and feeling pressured to do something about their child's behavior, find ways to justify their actions. They make those actions feel acceptable by convincing themselves that the child "deserved it" or that what they are doing is teaching the child a lesson he "needs to learn."

When you are questioning the way you are treating your child and are not sure if you are being fair, reasonable, and loving, or whether your behavior reflects your core values and life principles, replace yourself in your mind with another adult and "watch" him or her treating your child that way. Ask yourself:

- Would I like it if someone (you can insert the person's name if you choose to) was treating my child this way?
- Would I allow (insert name) to treat my child this way?
- What would I say to (insert name) if he/she was treating my child this way?

If at least one of your answers to these questions is "no," you are probably not responding as you would if you were truly connected with yourself.

13. Assign a better meaning. You cannot control your child and how she behaves. Parenting situations often cannot be controlled by you either. What you can control, however, is what meaning you assign to your child's behavior or the situation. When you feel worried, angry, or scared, those feelings are indicators that you are assigning to the child's behavior or the situation a meaning that causes you to feel that way. Instead, ask yourself the question that I learned at one of the seminars I attended by the life coach and business strategist Tony Robbins—"What else could this mean?"

Imagine you did not allow your child to play outside, play video games, or continue with her favorite activity because it was dinner time. Your child got frustrated with you and began saying mean things to you. You have a choice here. You can make what she says mean that she is being spiteful and get angry with her. Alternatively, you can ask yourself, "What else could this mean?" and realize that it could mean that your child is not yet able to handle "no" in a more appropriate way and needs more explicit teaching and guidance from you.

When you choose the latter, you will feel more compassion and determination to teach your child how to handle "no" in a way that feels respectful to you. It does not mean that you need to teach your child right then and there. You may want to wait until she is not upset with you anymore and then, in a loving and respectful way, discuss with her, using a neutral, confident tone of voice, other responses that she can choose from. Remember, there is more than one meaning that is available to you. Select the one that will help you connect with yourself and with your child the most.

14. "Name it to tame it." Use Dr. Siegal's strategy mentioned in Chapter 5 to connect with yourself by becoming aware of your feelings. Ask yourself, "What am I feeling right now?" Name the emotion you feel to help yourself calm down by allowing yourself to feel heard, "I hear you. I know how you feel. "

When you have a hard time calming down, you will most likely experience additional emotions, such as guilt, anger, or disappointment with yourself for feeling that emotion. For example, you may feel angry with your child and feel guilty at the same time for feeling angry with your child. This happens when you believe that you should not feel the way you feel. In moments like this, remind yourself that it is alright to feel what you feel. For example, "I feel angry with my child, and feeling angry is ok." Instead of resisting, allow yourself to experience that emotion without acting on it.

15. Respect your child's "model of the world."[5]
Based on our experiences and interpretation of them, we form a model of the world. Although the world is the way it is, each of us sees it differently. That is why one's perception of it is just a model, and different people have different models.

When you insist that your model of the world is correct, you deny your child's model of the world. In reality, no one's model of the world is completely correct, just like no one's model of the world is completely incorrect. We feel more compassionate and open to the child's perspective when we respect and do our best to understand her world model. Instead of arguing with your child and trying to prove why you are right, and she's wrong, make an effort to learn as much as you can about her model of the world by asking her questions, such as:

- What are you thinking right now?
- What caused you to think that?

- How do you see the situation?
- Can you explain to me what happened from your perspective?

16. Lead by example. Remind yourself that you are your child's leader, teacher, and guide. Your child learns from you by observing you and mirroring your behavior. You are her role model. If you want to build a strong connection with your child, learn, and then show with your actions how to connect with yourself in order to calm down, make rational decisions, and behave in the way you feel proud of.

Use feeling strong emotions to your advantage. See them as a signal to become aware of how those emotions affect your actions. Ask yourself, "Am I being the role model I want to be for my child?" or "What lesson am I teaching my child when I am behaving this way?" The good news is that it is never too late to change your behavior if you do not like the answer.

17. "Interview" visualization. Imagine that your child becomes extremely successful when she grows up and gives an interview with a popular news show. She is being asked to describe the moment she remembers the most from childhood, and she chooses to describe the events that are taking place right now. Ask yourself the following questions:

- Why did my child remember this moment so vividly?
- What kind of impact did I make on my child by how I handled this situation?
- What would she say about this moment?
- What emotions would she have experienced at this moment?
- What would she tell the journalist about me as a parent?

- How would she describe my behavior at this moment?
- What kind of emotions would she experience when talking about this moment?

18. Seize the moment. Parents are often intimidated by their child's challenging behavior. They think of a conflict as a moment of disconnection in their parent-child relationship and often contemplate its negative long-term effect. While it is important to consider your parenting's long-term impact on your child, a stressful situation is not the time to have those thoughts. Thoughts of that nature cause feelings of anxiety, stress, and fear, often leading to parents reacting out of fear by applying one of the F3 responses.

Instead of running those dreadful thoughts in your mind, think, "This is my opportunity to connect with my child." When your child is displaying challenging behavior, she needs to feel connected to and supported by you. She needs you to be there for her. "What about those moments when my child gets upset with me and tells me to leave?" you may be wondering. Children often say that and rarely mean it. They often say that when they don't know how to tell you or are too embarrassed to tell you how much they need you at that moment. By pushing you away, your child wants to show you how upset she is and hopes that you, as a parent, will understand and stay with her to help her handle her emotions and the situation better.

When it does seem to the child that having you leave is what she wants, it does not mean that you cannot connect with her. You can still connect with her by making yourself available. You can let your child know that you will check on her in a few minutes and leave her alone, let her know where you are going to be, so she can come to find you whenever she is ready, or you can do both.

The truth is that when your child is being the most "difficult," that's when she needs you the most. These moments are opportunities for you to be there for her and let her know how much you care. In the child's world, full of uncertainty, she wants to feel certain that she can count on you to be there for her, even if sometimes it means that you are temporarily a few feet or yards away. Even when physically distanced, you will still be emotionally connected. After you come back together, you can strengthen your emotional connection. It does not have to happen right when emotions are running high; wait until you are both emotionally ready to connect.

19. "10-10-10 technique." I learned about this strategy from Susie Welsh's book *10-10-10*. When dealing with a challenging situation in which she had to make a tough decision, Susie Welsh has taught herself to ask, "What are the consequences of my decision in 10 minutes, 10 months, and 10 years?"[6]

One of the examples that the author gave was when she had to decide whether to go home because she promised her children that she would see them at dinner and avoid having her children get upset, or stay at work to solve the crisis that erupted unexpectedly and later get a promotion so that she could be a better provider. She asked herself the consequences of her decision in ten minutes, ten months, and ten years if she decided to stay at work. She acknowledged that the children would still be upset in 10 minutes, they would be fine in 10 months, and they would not even remember that one late night at the office in 10 years.

20. "Begin with the end in mind." In *The Seven Habits of Highly Effective People*, Stephen Covey prompted the reader to participate in an exercise where he asked the reader to imagine herself going to the funeral of a loved one.[7] I would like to guide you through a slightly adjusted version of this exercise.

Imagine attending a funeral. As you walk to the casket, you see your family members' remorseful faces, notice the flowers, and hear the moving organ music. When you come closer to the casket, you suddenly see yourself inside and realize that this is *your* funeral and that all of those people came to honor you. You take a seat and listen to four speakers. One of them is your child. Answer the following questions:

- What would you like your child to say about you as a parent?
- What moments do you hope she shares about spending time with you?
- What lessons do you hope she shares that she learned from you?
- What impact do you hope you made on how she is now?
- What do you hope she would be grateful to you for?
- Would she feel proud of being your child?

Finding Peace through Practice

When used regularly, these strategies will help you stay self-connected and make decisions from the place of love, even in the most challenging parenting situations. You don't have to apply every single one of them. They are more like items on the shelves at the store—you can choose what you feel is right for you. Apply the strategies, choose the ones that work best for you, and begin noticing the difference in how you feel and how you respond in challenging parenting situations.

When you are in a self-connected state, you can help your

child connect with herself. When she is connected with herself, she will feel more connected to you. Learn how to help your child connect with herself by using the steps I share in the following chapter.

Staying Self-Connected Action Step

Begin strengthening your connection with your child by applying the strategies from this chapter. Go to your *Parenting Connection Workbook* and complete the exercises to determine what strategies you will commit to using to be able to respond from a peaceful and loving place.

8

HELPING YOUR CHILD PROCESS EMOTIONS

During my first home visit to Aimee's house as a family relationship coach, she and I were conversing at the dinner table while her four-year-old daughter Caroline sat on her lap, eating a snack. Suddenly, Caroline jumped off Aimee's lap and headed toward the fridge. This type of behavior was clearly common because it looked like Aimee knew exactly what her daughter was up to. Aimee immediately got up with an anxious look on her face and quickly followed her daughter while trying to look calm and poised.

Caroline approached the fridge, opened the freezer, and, smiling at us, triumphantly raised an ice cream bar above her head.

"It's not dessert time yet," said Aimee, nervously but gently taking the ice cream bar out of Caroline's hand and putting it back in the freezer. Caroline's face became red with anger. Glaring right into her mother's eyes, she looked ready to burst out screaming.

Embarrassed by Caroline's behavior, but also not wanting her daughter to be upset, Aimee quickly walked toward the window, pulled up the blinds, and chattered in the sweetest voice she could squeeze out of her anxious self, "Sweetie, did you see the birdie outside? He's so cute! Right there in the tree."

In a rage, Caroline yelled back, "I don't want to look at the stupid birdie!"

"Oh, sweetheart, don't say that! It's not nice to call the birdie stupid. It's not nice to call anyone…"

"He's stupid! Stupid! Stupid!" interrupted Caroline, getting even more aggravated.

Bewildered and panicked, Aimee stood there, not knowing what to do. To help, I decided to intervene.

"You look angry, Caroline. Is that how you are feeling?" I asked.

Caroline instantly switched from angry to scared. She ran up to her mother and hid behind her. Peeking out from behind her mother, she looked at me as if I asked a forbidden question. Aimee put her hand over Caroline's shoulder and squeezed her tight as if she was trying to protect her daughter. They both stood there with puzzled and anxious looks on their faces. I could immediately tell by their reaction that discussing "negative" feelings was taboo in their home.

The reality is that their home is not the only one where feelings are something family members don't talk about. Learning how to discuss and process emotions is not part of the school curriculum or common in our society. Yet, we are expected to somehow know how to handle our emotions in healthy and productive ways. Most of us figured it out much later in life, after having endured a lot of unnecessary emotional suffering that could have been avoided if we learned how to deal with our emotions at a young age.

Accepting Our Emotions

Designed to protect us, the primal brain causes us to want to avoid what hurts us physically or emotionally. Unpleasant feelings seem to hurt, so the primal brain is afraid of them. It believes that unpleasant feelings are too much for us to handle, and therefore, causes us to avoid them. It does not understand that when we avoid, resist, or deny our feelings, we avoid, resist, and deny ourselves, which becomes the source of emotional suffering.

Teaching your child to allow, accept, and process his emotions will help him avoid emotional suffering and feel connected with himself and you. The skill of processing his feelings is the most remarkable gift you can give to your child.

The following is my gift to you and your child—a step-by-step approach for you to teach your child to allow, accept, and process his emotions. These steps are based on my personal and professional experiences, as well as inspired by insights from experts in the field of neuroscience, family therapy, parenting, psychology, psychiatry, personal development, communication, and emotional intelligence, such as Virginia Satir, Cloé Madanes, Daniel Goleman, John Gottman, Geneen Roth, Mark Goulston, Adele Faber, Elaine Mazlish, Haim Ginott, and Daniel J. Siegel.

Once your child learns how to process his feelings, he will feel empowered, more confident, and connected to himself. Being able to deal with any feeling in a healthy way will enable your child to consciously and purposefully respond to even the most difficult life challenges from the place of self-connectedness, confidence, and love.

These steps are not another set of rules or procedures for you to strictly follow—you already have enough of those! Use them as your GPS, knowing that whichever route you choose, using them will lead you to the desired destination. Experiment, play with them, have fun. Choose what works best for your unique situation and parent-child relationship.

Make sure to give yourself and your child time; do not rush through the process. If you feel like you are short on time, wait to implement these steps later in the day or the following day. This process is a deeply connecting experience that requires your complete presence—physical, mental, emotional, and spiritual.

It is important to explore both pleasant and unpleasant feelings in order to get to know ourselves better. All feelings serve a purpose and are worth exploring. Before you start applying these steps to help your child explore and process his strong, unpleasant feelings, you may choose to practice using them with pleasant ones to ease yourself and your child into these new experiences. The more the practice of exploring pleasant feelings becomes familiar to your child, the less effort it will take for him to apply these steps when processing his unpleasant feelings.

Teach your child to be present with his unpleasant feelings. Avoid the mistake of trying to protect your child from experiencing them by using different tactics like distracting your child, telling him to calm down, or convincing him that what he is crying about isn't important. By guiding your child through the following steps, you will teach him to use the power of his brain to think in a way that will help him become emotionally intelligent, confident, and fulfilled.

Ten Steps to Helping Your Child Process Emotions

1. Connect with yourself. Self-connect by becoming aware of and honoring your own thoughts and feelings. If you are not feeling ready and confident in your ability to guide your child through his emotions successfully, your thoughts are the reason why. Use the Parenting Success Formula to change your thoughts and feelings by asking yourself, "What am I thinking right now?" Then move into the place of love, confidence, and calmness by taking time to consider, "What can I choose to think at this moment to help myself feel calm, connected, and able to guide my child from a place of love?" Use the strategies in Chapter 7 to connect with who you really are.

2. Become aware of your child's emotions. Once you are in a peaceful, connected state yourself, you can focus on your child's emotion by asking yourself, "What is my child feeling right now?" Do your best to become aware of your child's emotions by simply observing him or using the strategies in Chapter 7 that will help you feel compassion for your child and understand how he feels.

Honor and respect his feelings. Whatever he feels, take his feelings seriously, even if you think that the reason is trivial. It may seem trivial from your perspective as an adult, but it may be a big deal for your child. If you are having a hard time taking his feelings seriously, remember how big of a deal some things were to you when you were a child that adults in your life considered insignificant, such as your teacher calling on you when you did not know the answer, a drawing not turning out the way you wanted, or falling down in front of your peers.

3. Describe what you see without judgment. Describing what you see without judgment helps your child understand the situation better and see it more objectively and establish a correspondence between his emotion and its physical manifestation through his facial expressions and body language. Understanding how he looks when experiencing a certain emotion will increase your child's self- and social awareness.

You can use observational phrases, such as "I have noticed that...," "Your face looks...," "I see that you are..." when describing your child's expression of his emotions. For example, "I see that you look embarrassed. Your face is red, and you are looking down at the ground," or "I noticed that since you got from the daycare today, you have not been playing with your favorite dolls as you usually do. You've just been sitting quietly on the floor looking out the window."

4. Name the emotion. In stressful, highly emotional situations, ask your child, "How are you feeling?" If he doesn't know the word for the emotion, you can help him name the emotion. As you've already learned, by naming the emotion, you help your child integrate the left and right hemispheres, which decreases feelings of fear and anxiety and helps him calm down.

Because the primal brain does not like unfamiliarity, it is afraid of what it does not understand and sees it as a potential threat. Not understanding what is happening in his body and not being able to name the emotion or express his feelings may increase the child's anxiety and fear. Your child will naturally want to resist the unpleasant emotion because it doesn't feel good. Resisting the emotion may only cause more physical and emotional tension, leading to more distress, discomfort, and increased intensity of the emotion. Naming the emotion is one of the ways to reduce or even prevent this distress and discomfort.

Another goal that naming your child's emotion accomplishes is it helps the child to enrich his emotional vocabulary. Being familiar with the way each emotion feels in his body and identifying it with the corresponding word empowers your child to express himself accurately and clearly, takes away the fear for the brain confusion and the unknown, and releases the inner tension.

If both you and your child struggle to identify what he is feeling, do not feel pressured to name the emotion, just continue with another one of the steps. If you want to focus on helping your child to explore his feelings, consider step 7. Exploring his feelings even without naming them can have a powerful calming effect on your child and lead to self-connecting experiences. It's another way for the brain to become familiar with what is happening in the child's body, allow, and accept it.

5. Listen. REALLY listen. In *The 7 Habits of Highly Effective People*, Stephen R. Covey wrote, "Most people do not listen with the intent to understand; they listen with the intent to reply."[1] When most parents hear this quote, they immediately think, "Yes, that's exactly what my husband (wife, mother, father, friend) does, but it has nothing to do with me." If that is what you believe, I encourage you to reconsider and take a closer look. We often overestimate our listening skills when we are stressed, worried, or anxious.

I want you to become curious and simply observe yourself next time you have a conversation with your child. Ask yourself, "Am I listening to understand or waiting to respond?" Most adults cannot wait to talk. Because we have more experience, it is usually easier for us to find a solution. To help their child feel better, parents naturally want to "fix" the child's problem by immediately giving a piece of advice or offering a solution.

Remember the last time you were having strong emotions and just wanted to share with someone? The last thing you wanted was to be given advice ("So, here is what you need to do..."), a philosophical response ("Trust me, you won't even remember it when you reach my age."), or a shameful comment ("I can't believe you did that!"). All you wanted was somebody just to listen to you without any judgment or criticism, with a genuine intent to understand. You wanted to, as Mark Goulston describes in his book *Just Listen*, "feel felt."[2] So does your child.

When he is having a hard time, it is an opportunity for you to help him feel better by attentively and respectfully listening. To show your empathy and engagement, you may choose to nod, smile (if appropriate), or comment, "Oh," "Ok," "I see."

You do not have to agree or act as if you agree if you have a different opinion. All you need to do is give them time and your full attention and listen. Just listen.

6. Hold space for your child's emotions. Allow your child to feel the unpleasant emotion instead of attempting to stop it or immediately switching to a different, pleasant emotion. There are two mistakes that parents often make when attempting to help their child feel better. One mistake is trying to distract the child. Parents believe that by distracting their child, they can stop the child's emotional suffering. What they do not realize is that by doing that, they do more harm than good.

Firstly, they inadvertently teach the child that distraction is a solution to strong emotions. When the child learns to look for distractions every time he experiences strong unpleasant emotions, he misses an opportunity to practice processing his emotions. Additionally, those distractions may eventually become the child's addictions, such as excessively playing video games, overeating, and alcohol or drug abuse.

Secondly, distracting the child from feeling his emotions is only a temporary solution. The child may forget about his feelings for now, but he will also miss a chance to properly process his emotions. When not fully processed, those strong emotions come back sooner or later. When they come back, they are often even stronger, and your child may not be ready to handle them.

Another mistake parents make is immediately switching the child's strong unpleasant emotions to pleasant ones. In doing so, parents unintentionally put pressure on their child. The child might not be ready to replace his unpleasant feelings with pleasant ones and feel embarrassed, ashamed, or guilty for not meeting his parents' expectations. He may even learn to suppress or hide his emotions and pretend to feel differently than he does instead of learning to process them in a healthy way.

Holding space for your child's unpleasant emotions and letting them stay until fully processed will allow your child to experience his emotions without feeling the pressure to feel differently. Treat his feelings with reverence and compassion. If he is crying, allow him to cry. If he feels sad, allow him to feel sad. Trying to immediately stop his emotions or replace them with more pleasant emotions is a superficial and temporal "fix." These emotions will dispel when given space to be fully processed.

7. Help your child explore his feelings. When we want to become friends with someone, we become curious and take our time to get to know them. The same is true about feelings. If you want your child to feel comfortable with his feelings, teach him to get to know his feelings. His feelings guide him and let him know what's important to him and whether he is being true to himself or needs to make different decisions and take different actions. To help your child explore his feelings, use the questions below, some of which I learned from Richard Bandler's work on Neuro-Linguistic Programming, including *Get the Life You Want*, and some of which I derived from Geneen Roth's work *When Food is Food & Love is Love*.[3] [4]

Ask your child to describe the feeling:

- Where is the feeling in your body?
- Is it moving, or is it still? (If he says the feeling is moving, ask him how it's moving, e.g., fast or slow, up or down, forward or backward.)
- Does the feeling have a shape, temperature, or color?

- What shape is your feeling? What temperature is it? What color is it?

Describing his feelings can help your child be more open to feeling and discussing his emotions, instead of acting on them. Taking time to feel an emotion in his body, such as by exploring where it is, what shape, color, size, and texture it is, can help your child remain self-connected when experiencing strong emotions.

I also highly recommend teaching your child about emotion being a message and help him develop curiosity about what his emotions are teaching him. You may guide him by asking the following questions:

- What message do you think your emotion is sending you?
- What do you think this emotion wants you to know about yourself? (The answer might be, "I do not like to be treated that way," or "This person's relationship is important to me.")
- What lesson do you think this emotion wants you to learn from this situation?

Explain to your child that by asking himself these questions, he gets an opportunity to get to know himself better, learn what's important to him, and identify what he wants in life. When he knows himself better and what's important to him, he will be able to consciously make the changes he wants in order to be able to create his dream life while staying true to himself.

8. Discuss the learned lessons and review the family values and principles. This is an optional step that may not be applicable to all situations. Take into consideration why your child is experiencing the emotion and consider if a lesson needs to be learned at that specific moment. For example, when your child is grieving over the recent loss of his pet, talking about learned lessons or family values may not be appropriate in this situation or at this specific time. Additionally, before implementing this step, consider whether you already have established and mutually agreed upon family values and principles.

When taking this step, give your child the opportunity to voice his opinion. Once you have heard what your child has to say, remind him of what your family values and principles are. Help him understand how what he did was not aligned with those values and principles. Then, discuss with him what could be a more appropriate way of expressing his emotions if the same or a similar situation were to occur.

When you need to establish or re-establish principles, demonstrate the behavior for your child to help him understand better and be more successful in implementing the principles you agree upon. Keep it neutral and use "we" instead of "you" when appropriate to avoid sounding accusatory. For example, let's say the child was not behaving politely when you had friends over. Instead of saying, "You have to be more polite when hosting guests," you can say, "To help our guests feel more welcome, let's agree as a family to have this principle: be polite when hosting guests." Clearly explain to the child what "being polite" means and looks like. You can begin by asking him what he thinks "being polite" means and demonstrate to you what it looks like. If you notice that he is confused or needs additional clarification, demonstrate how to do it. Role-playing is one of the ways you can make learning fun for both of you.

If you have not yet taught your child how to treat you, then use this step to set your personal boundaries, so that your child has clear guidelines going forward. You will learn more about setting boundaries in the next chapter.

9. Share with your child how you feel. Many parents avoid sharing their so-called "negative" emotions with their children because they don't want their children to worry, feel guilty, or see their parents as weak. By suppressing their emotions, parents cause a lot of issues for themselves and their children sooner or later.

One of the most common issues that parents begin to notice first is that their child becomes insensitive and indifferent to his parents' feelings. This happens because when parents hide their emotions, the child may think that his actions do not affect them or his parents simply do not care. He may also believe that because the people he looks up to don't show or talk about their emotions, it is not appropriate to show or talk about emotions and learn to hide them.

The truth is that when done appropriately, sharing your feelings with your child can be a powerful connecting experience in your parent-child relationship. With a supportive, kind, and serious voice, help your child understand your emotional reaction to his actions. Avoid blaming, belittling, or shaming, and make it clear to your child that it is his actions that you have unpleasant emotions about, not him as a person. Also, remember that your child is free to feel whatever emotion he is experiencing at the moment. His emotions are never the issue. The challenge lies in his behavior choices, i.e., his responses to the emotion, when these choices are doing a disservice to him or others. When appropriate, reassure him that you love and *will* love him no matter what.

Sharing your emotions helps your child connect with you more through understanding your perspective and emotions better, which, in turn, enhances the child's ability to feel compassion and increases his social awareness.

10. Teach your child to find a solution. Teaching your child to find a solution does not mean finding a solution for him, but rather guiding him through the process, using what he has learned from the situation, and his experiences in this situation to find a solution. Children are natural problem solvers. When working on finding a solution with your child, encourage his input, and allow him to feel that his voice matters.

Ten Steps to Helping Your Child Process Emotions in Action

Here is how Isabella put the Ten Steps to Helping Your Child Process Emotions into practice. Her ten-year-old son Samuel had gotten into a fight at school with his best friend, Adrian. Samuel got angry with Adrian for getting him into trouble. At lunch, Adrian threw food on the cafeteria floor and didn't admit it when the cafeteria worker asked who did it. She thought it was Samuel and asked him to pick it up. Samuel told her he didn't do it, and angrily refused to follow her directions. The cafeteria worker didn't believe him and had him stay during recess to help clean the cafeteria. Samuel was so angry with Adrian for letting him take the blame that he pushed Adrian when he saw his friend after lunch. Adrian pushed back, and the fight began...

When Samuel arrived home from school, he was still feeling outraged. Hearing Samuel calling his best friend names, seeing him breaking the handmade wooden airplane that Adrian gave him as a gift, and ripping his favorite photo of the two of them, Isabella became scared. She had never seen her son in such a rage. She felt an urge to immediately step in and tell him to calm down and that everything was going to be alright because he and Adrian will be best friends again soon.

Isabella paused upon remembering what she learned

about the brain, the Parenting Success Formula, and the Ten Steps to Helping Your Child Process Emotions. She realized that she was not ready to help her son because she was in a state of fear. She was worried and anxious about her son's behavior and could end up reacting instead of consciously responding to the situation. So, she decided to connect with herself first in order to be able to help her son process his emotions.

Step 1. Connect with yourself. Isabella asked herself, "What am I thinking right now?" She realized she was thinking about how much Samuel was hurting. She was telling herself that her son would never be able to trust anyone again. Although caring and empathetic, her thoughts weren't helpful. Isabella understood that continuing to think those thoughts would cause her to feel even more anxious.

The next question she asked herself was, "What can I choose to think instead to help myself feel calm and self-connected?" Isabella chose to think, "It is true that I might not know how to help my son right now, but it's ok. I'm just going to give Samuel space and then help him connect with himself by guiding him through the emotion processing steps. Then, together, we will figure something out." Taking this step helped Isabella become calmer, more confident, and present. Now, she was ready to support her son better.

Step 2. Become aware of your child's emotions. Once she felt self-connected, Isabella could pay better attention to and become more aware of Samuel's emotions. It allowed her to notice when Samuel was ready to talk to her.

. . .

Step 3. Describe what you see without judgment.
Then, she described what she saw without using judgmental comments, such as "Those were mean things to say about your best friend." Instead, Isabella said, "I see that your lips are tight, and your eyebrows are pulled down together. I also saw you ripping your favorite photo of the two of you and breaking Adrian's gift."

Step 4. Name the emotion. Isabella named the emotion, "We sometimes do things like that when we feel outraged. That's probably what you feel right now. You may also feel disappointed with what Adrian did."

Step 5. Listen. REALLY listen. Isabella then paused and let her son talk while she sat and listened. She listened attentively, without interrupting, showing with her facial expressions and head nods that she was giving Samuel her full attention and what her son said mattered to her.

Step 6. Hold space for your child's emotions. When Samuel was done talking, Isabella did not try to change his emotions by distracting him, cheering him up, or comforting her son. She held space for his emotions and gave him a chance to feel the way he did.

Step 7. Help your child explore his feelings. Next, when Samuel calmed down a little more after venting, Isabella helped Samuel explore his feelings by asking him, "Where is this feeling in your body? How does it feel? Does it feel warm or cold?"

. . .

Step 8. Discuss the learned lessons and review the family values and principles. After talking about his feelings and ensuring that Samuel allowed himself to feel them, Isabella reviewed the family values and principles with him. The family previously agreed that they valued kindness and respect, and one of their principles was that physical fighting was not acceptable under any circumstances. Instead of lecturing Samuel or restating the values and the principle, Isabella reviewed their values and principles by asking her son to tell her what they were.

Step 9. Share with your child how you feel. Next, Isabella explained how she felt, "When you fight, I worry about you. I don't want you to get hurt. I also worry about Adrian because he could have gotten hurt."

Step 10. Teach your child to find a solution. Lastly, Samuel and his mother discussed possible solutions. Isabella encouraged Sebastian to find a solution that he believed would work best for everyone involved. Samuel decided to apologize to Adrian for pushing him and write a letter of apology to the cafeteria worker. Samuel thanked his mother for her support and hugged her.

Of course, you may not see or hear these types of solutions from your child just yet, but if you regularly implement these steps, you may observe such behavior from him soon. You will notice a big change in your child's ability to deal with his emotions and your feeling of connection with him.

Connecting through Processing Emotions

I know that is a lot of information. However, you do not have to implement all of these steps in every situation. There may be times when only one or two steps are enough to help your child deal with his emotions. You may choose to skip some of these steps or take them out of order, depending on what works best for a particular situation, except for the first step—connecting with yourself.

Processing his feelings will help your child get to know himself by becoming familiar with how different emotions feel in his body and learn to move into a peaceful place when in stressful situations by allowing, naming, and feeling his emotions when they arise, instead of resisting, avoiding, or acting out on them. Implementing these steps is a profound way to develop a deep connection between you and your child.

Helping Your Child Process Emotions Action Step

Your *Parenting Connection Workbook* is filled with exercises and questions that will help you use the Ten Steps to Helping Your Child Process Emotions effectively to transform challenging moments into connecting moments. Visit www.albinspire. com/workbook to download your copy.

9

CONNECTING THROUGH BOUNDARIES

As an educator, having learned about the brain, children's needs, and emotions, I noticed that connecting with any student was only a matter of time for me. Being able to understand thoughts and reasons for a child's behavior, I felt unconditionally loving and compassionate. My students and I greatly enjoyed an overall peaceful and joyful environment. However, there was one more aspect that was still confusing to me and caused me emotional suffering. I could not understand why some of my students I had a connection with would sometimes choose to take what I was doing for them for granted and treat me in less than respectful ways—until a new nine-year-old student, Amina, helped me figure it out.

Before Amina arrived at our school, I had been told that the student had a history of abuse and neglect prior to moving to the United States. Without having met Amina yet, I felt deep compassion for her and was committed to doing whatever it took to make sure that Amina's experiences at her new school and new country were positive.

From the moment I met Amina in the office, I was as friendly, nice, and welcoming as possible. I really wanted

Amina to be happy and feel comfortable around adults and see them as trustworthy and kind. Gradually, I was able to develop some connection and trust in our student-teacher relationship.

Blindly following my commitment to make Amina happy, I found justifications for her inappropriate behavior. Whenever Amina would break school supplies, laugh in my face, tell me she would not listen to me, or threaten to hit me or hurt somebody else, I would not get frustrated or angry with her. Instead, I would feel even more empathy for her and try to make up for how the adults in her life had treated her. I made her happiness my priority.

I was consumed with worry about Amina. I would go home and cry, wondering what else I could do to make her happy and get her interested in learning so that she would have the skills and knowledge she needed to do whatever she wanted in life. Although I genuinely cared about Amina, deep inside, I was also terrified of working with her because I never knew what to expect. She could be laughing with me and doing everything I asked of her during one class and meet me with the most derogatory remarks or refuse to even acknowledge my presence fifteen minutes later in the next class. I felt hurt, unappreciated, disrespected, and immensely embarrassed when she put me down in front of others. I spent hours constantly reflecting, thinking, and planning how to approach Amina in a way that would help her not overreact. At the start of each day, I desperately hoped she would be in a good mood, listen, and behave, but usually, that wasn't the case.

On a usual day, an unusual event became a wake-up call from the frightening nightmare I was living in. It was raining, so students had indoor recess. I was working in the room I shared with other specialists when suddenly, the silence was broken by the door swinging wide open and hitting the door stopper. Amina's angry face appeared. She yelled at me,

"Come here! Right now!" Before I got a chance to ask her what had happened, she was already gone. Concerned, I quickly got up and followed her. When I went out into the hallway, Amina was already halfway back to her classroom. She turned around and waved at me to follow along, as a master would to his dog, and yelled again, "Hurry up! I'm running out of time!"

I sped up. I was walking as fast as I could. Behind my back, I heard my colleagues who were standing in the hallway next to my room door and witnessed what happened, saying to another, "What an attitude! I would never let a student talk to me that way!" I felt embarrassed about Amina's behavior (I really wanted her to behave well so that everyone liked and thought well of her) and about myself being wrapped around her finger and doing whatever she wanted me to do to avoid her getting upset.

When I arrived at Amina's classroom, she stood there with her arms crossed, righteously looking down at the two girls playing chess. "I want to play with them, but they don't want to. Tell them that one of them has to play with me right now," she ordered. The girls looked intimidated by Amina's behavior. I stood there, hesitant about what to do. I knew I should advocate for the girls and teach Amina that the way she spoke was not appropriate. At the same time, I was afraid of breaking the connection I had built with her so far. I reasoned that although she treated me with disrespect, she still chose to ask *me* for help.

Standing there, indecisively shifting my focus back and forth between the girls and Amina, I thought, "Did I create this monstrous behavior by always trying to please her? Did I teach this girl to think that it was acceptable to treat others this way? Did I lead her to believe that she was entitled to always get what she wanted, even when at the expense of others?" Without much time to contemplate and with Amina getting agitated, I knew I had to do something. I was afraid that if I didn't, she was going to become aggressive toward the girls.

I came up to the girls and nicely asked if one of them could play just one match with Amina. Unwillingly, but uncomfortable with saying "no" to me, one of them agreed.

That night, my confusing thoughts and feelings of guilt, embarrassment, and disappointment with myself would not leave me alone. I must not have been good at hiding it because, when my sister saw me, she asked me what happened. "I must be doing something wrong," I replied. "I want what's best for this student. I want to teach her to respect and be kind to others, so she could have healthy, fulfilling relationships. But it seems like nothing works."

Concerned about how I was allowing myself to be treated, my sister asked, "How can you teach the child to respect you and others if you do not respect yourself?" I was shocked and even slightly resented my sister's response. My immediate reaction was to disagree and prove her wrong, but, knowing how much my sister loved and cared for me, I knew she would not say anything to hurt my feelings and only wanted to help. I paused and thought about her question. It became clear to me that she was right. I did not respect myself. If I did, I would not allow myself to be treated the way Amina treated me. I realized the mistake I'd made—I avoided taking care of myself by setting and honoring my personal boundaries. No wonder Amina treated me the way she did.

The next day, I met with Amina and set my first boundary. I reassured her that I was there for her and was happy to help. I also explained to her that I would not come out if she asked me for help the way she did previously. If she wanted my help, she needed to politely knock on the door before opening it, say, "Hello," and ask if I was available to talk to her. Amina didn't seem to like it, but seeing me being firm with her for the first time, agreed. That initial boundary became my first step to a mutually respectful, trusting, and emotionally connected relationship with Amina.

Two Major Mistakes in Boundary Setting

There are two significant mistakes that parents make when setting boundaries. I know because I've made them both. We often set and maintain boundaries in an unhealthy or ineffective way (like I used to do when I just began teaching) or avoid setting or honoring boundaries altogether (my approach until my experience with Amina). What you will learn in this chapter will help you eliminate both mistakes.

Why We Avoid Setting and Honoring Personal Boundaries

My reflection on my experience with Amina helped me understand why I had been avoiding setting and honoring personal boundaries. Later, when I began observing and coaching parents, I realized that I wasn't the only one struggling with this for those same reasons. The following are the main reasons why establishing boundaries is so difficult.

One is that many of us don't even know what our boundaries are. As children, we were not taught to identify how we wanted to be treated, let alone how to set and teach others how to treat us by honoring our boundaries.

What were we taught instead? We were taught to share even when we didn't feel like sharing, hug people when we didn't feel like hugging, and force ourselves to have conversations when we just wanted to be left alone. We unwittingly were trained not to trust our own feelings, perceptions, and needs and to prioritize those of the people around us. We were taught to be nice, even when it was at our own expense. As a result, we have mistakenly inferred that in order to be nice, we must not have or disregard our boundaries when others don't like them so as not to upset them. This is the second reason why we avoid having and honoring personal boundaries.

Thirdly, based on our past experiences with people setting and honoring their boundaries in aggressive, inappropriate ways, such as demanding, yelling, or punishing others, we mistakenly learned that setting and honoring boundaries must be accompanied by anger, fear, embarrassment, or other strong unpleasant feelings. To avoid those unpleasant feelings or come across as aggressive or mean, we often decide to avoid having boundaries altogether.

Finally, we all want to connect by feeling appreciated, loved, and accepted. We are afraid of establishing boundaries because we mistakenly believe that connections and boundaries are mutually exclusive. Needing connection and perceiving setting and honoring boundaries as a disconnecting experience, parents chose to avoid having boundaries in their parent-child relationship.

The truth is that having and honoring your boundaries is the basis of a strong connection in a parent-child relationship. When parents avoid setting, consistently honoring, and teaching the child to honor their personal boundaries, they often end up controlling, resenting, or punishing the child.

What Are Personal Boundaries?

Setting personal boundaries requires first understanding what they are. There is a common misconception about boundaries in a parent-child relationship. They are seen as the limits parents impose on the child in order to control his behavior. This interpretation of boundaries causes parents to focus on the child's behavior and ways to "fix" it. However, setting boundaries is not about creating rules or limits for your child. Personal boundaries are guidelines, rules or limits that a person creates to identify reasonable, safe and permissible ways for other people to behave towards them and how they will respond when someone passes those limits.[1]

Five Steps to Setting Personal Boundaries in a Healthy and Effective Way

The better your child knows what your boundaries are, understands your reasons for setting them, and learns how to honor them, the easier it will be for him to do so, and the easier it will be for the two of you to build a stronger connection.

The following are five steps to setting personal boundaries in a healthy and effective way. Implementing these five steps will help you teach your child how to treat you. It will also give you an opportunity to get to know yourself better and enjoy your parent-child relationship more. Keep in mind that the best practice in boundary-setting is doing it when you and your child feel calm and connected, not during stressful parenting situations.

Step 1. Connect with yourself to identify your personal boundaries. In order to set your boundaries, you first need to identify what they are by connecting with yourself and answering these questions:

- What am I comfortable with?
- How do I want to be treated by my child?
- How do I not want to be treated by my child?

When answering these questions, many parents tend to look outside themselves. They look to see what other parents are doing and what society tells them about how children should behave. The problem with that is when they adopt other people's boundaries or base their boundaries on common beliefs rather than their own values, life principles, and inner convictions, they often end up disappointed and unhappy.

You can avoid making this mistake by connecting with yourself and listening to your heart and mind in order to find out what's important to *you* and how you would like to be treated. Only you know the answer to those questions. Only you can decide what personal boundaries to have in your parent-child relationship. That is why they are called personal —they are unique to every person.

Step 2. Clearly communicate your boundaries. To be able to honor your boundaries, the child first needs to know what they are. It is vital to communicate your boundaries clearly. The more ambiguity you can eliminate and the more clarity you can provide, the more you reduce your child's chance of guessing or misunderstanding your boundary. Removing uncertainty in setting personal boundaries is just like removing uncertainty in setting physical boundaries. For example, you would not want to leave your overnight guest wondering, "Is this my room or your room?" You would communicate which room is hers and which one is yours.

To communicate your boundaries clearly, use the words that you are sure your child understands and explain the meaning of the words you use that you think he may not know. For example, if the child takes your belongings without permission, you may say, "If you want to take something that belongs to me, I want you to ask me for permission. Permission means you ask the person if you are allowed to take something that belongs to them." To leave no room for ambiguity, ask your child if he has any questions or needs any further explanation to understand what you mean. If the child tells you he understood everything, ask him to tell you what he understood about the boundary you taught him. If the child tells you he did not understand, ask him what part he did not understand. Explain it to him again, in different ways, until he demonstrates that he completely understands the boundary you are teaching him.

Using an appropriate tone of voice is important when setting and communicating your boundaries. Even the most clearly communicated boundaries can be ineffective if you choose an inappropriate tone of voice. Many parents make a mistake by using either too high or too low a tone of voice when setting personal boundaries. They do not realize that using a too high tone of voice may cause them to sound insecure, anxious, or incompetent, which may result in the child not taking what they are saying seriously or even getting annoyed by the parent.

On the other hand, using a too low tone of voice may cause the child to feel scared or intimidated by the parent, resulting in the child shutting down and not perceiving what the parent is saying and in a weakened connection. Using a neutral, confident tone of voice while coming from a place of love will help your child understand that what you say is serious and important, which results in them paying better attention.

Step 3. Explain your reason for setting the boundary.
When you clearly explain to the child why you choose to set a boundary, you help your child understand you better and teach your child how to communicate openly and effectively. Setting boundaries often requires you to act differently than you usually do. When you change the way you respond to your child's behavior by having a more serious facial expression or using a different tone of voice than usual, your child may not understand the reason for the sudden change and may feel confused, take it personally, or misinterpret the changes as you not loving him anymore.

When three-year-old Nathan's mother Kara decided to set boundaries with him, instead of raising her voice and repeatedly telling him to stop as she usually did, she calmly told him that she would take his computer away if he continued pounding on the keyboard. Nathan, perplexed with his mother's unusual response to his actions and firm and calm tone of voice, began crying. When Kara comforted him and asked him if he was ok, he told her that he thought she didn't love him anymore.

That is one reason why it's essential to let your child know that setting boundaries is not about *him* as a person. It's about *you* and how *you* want to be treated. You also need to reassure him that setting boundaries has nothing to do with your love for him. Help him understand that you love him unconditionally and always will. Help him understand that the ultimate reason you are setting and honoring your boundaries is to take care of yourself out of self-love, self-respect, and self-care so that you can create a healthy and fulfilling relationship with him. By explaining why having this boundary is important to you and how you feel when your boundary is honored and when your child dishonors it, you avoid blaming the child for "making you feel a certain way," take responsibility for your feelings and help your child not to take your setting boundaries with him personally.

Three Boundary-Setting Mistakes to Watch Out For

I want to caution you about a few mistakes that many parents make. While they *think* they are explaining their reasons for setting or resetting their boundaries, they often unintentionally end up justifying, apologizing, or stacking up their reasons. Here is how you can tell the difference:

1. Justifying your reasons. You will know that you are not explaining but are *justifying* your reasons if you find yourself trying to prove to your child that you deserve to have boundaries or fight to establish your boundaries. For example, comments like, "I have to stand up for myself and must be treated with respect," "You have no right to treat me this way!" or "You have to listen to me because I'm your parent" indicate that you are in a "fight" mode. Just like everyone else, you have the right to have boundaries. You don't have to prove it to anyone or fight for it. It is a given. You will also know that you are justifying and not explaining your reasons by how you feel. If you feel unpleasant feelings, such as guilt, fear, or anxiety, you are most likely not explaining but justifying your reasons for your boundary setting. You may feel that way because you believe that you are being mean to your child by setting a boundary, are worried about your child's reaction to it, or afraid of losing your child's love or weaken your connection because of the boundary you are setting.

Another common reason you may feel like you have to justify your boundary is self-doubt. When you are not sure if the boundary you are setting is "right" or is going to work, you use justification as a way to convince both your child and yourself that you have good reasons for setting the boundary. That is why it is especially important to use the first step—connect with yourself to identify your boundaries. Doing it in a quiet place before your conversation with the child will help you determine your boundaries and why you need to have them. You will feel more confident about explaining your boundaries and your reasons to your child.

2. Apologizing. When you find yourself feeling guilty or judging yourself for "doing this to your child," you may notice yourself apologizing to your child for setting your boundary, "I'm sorry, but I have to do it because I don't want to be treated this way." There is no need to feel guilty for doing what's best for you and your child. When setting boundaries, you are taking care of yourself and your child by eliminating emotional suffering caused by vague boundaries or their absence. You are also a role model for your child by teaching him the importance of taking care of himself in a relationship by setting boundaries.

3. Stacking up reasons. "I'm not ok with that, not only because..., but also... Besides, ..." Parents feel like they have to name as many reasons as possible to validate their decision to set boundaries. They also think that if those reasons don't sound extremely important, they don't count. The truth is that having one reason is already enough and just because you *feel* that you need to have that boundary to take care of yourself is already an important reason. For example, feeling uncomfortable when your child raises his voice when talking to you can be an important reason for you to set a personal boundary.

When you justify yourself, apologize, or stack up reasons for setting boundaries, you are coming from a place of fear —you are afraid of and trying to avoid the unpleasant emotions that you think setting boundaries is going to cause. When you are coming from a place of fear, your connection with yourself and your child weakens. In addition, justifying yourself, apologizing, or stacking up reasons gives your child the impression that you do not believe that your reasons are good enough. When your child gets that impression, they are more likely to begin to question and resist your boundaries, which may lead to further tension and connection weakening between the two of you.

Step 4. Let the child know how you are going to respond. It's important to decide for yourself and then let your child know what your response will be when he honors or dishonors your boundaries. It's not about what you will force *the child* to do to change his behavior. It's about what changes *you* will make with *your* behavior to take care of yourself. Take responsibility for your actions and avoid sounding accusatory or threatening by using a respectful tone of voice and "I" instead of "you" when informing your child of your actions. For example, instead of saying, "If you keep mocking me, you will go to your room," you can say, "I like playing with you, but I don't like being mocked. Could you please not mock me? If I keep being mocked, I will stop playing with you."

Deciding and letting the child know how you will respond helps him have a sense of certainty because he knows what to expect from you, which builds trust between the two of you and enhances your parent-child connection.

Step 5. Explicitly teach the child how to honor your boundaries. In other words, teach your child what he can do to strengthen his connection with you.

First, begin by asking your child to describe your new boundary and explain your reasons for setting it. By doing so, you will accomplish two goals: help your child remember the information better and use it as an opportunity to clarify any misunderstandings your child may have.

Next, to help your child understand how to honor your boundaries, you can show your child what it does and does not look like. For example, if you want your child to ask you nicely to help him with putting his toys away instead of demanding you to help him, you can say, "If you want me to help you put your toys away, I want to be asked this way, 'Dad, could you please help me to put my toys away?'"

If you think your child needs further clarification, practice with him by replaying what just happened or with scenarios that usually occur. Tell him that you will ask him again to put his toys away, but this time, instead of saying, "You have to help me!" he needs to say, "Dad, could you please help me put my toys away?"

Another way to explicitly teach your child to honor your boundaries would be role-playing, where you would pretend to be a child and show how you want to be asked for help in a way that sounds nice and respectful to you. Then, have your child do the same by telling him, "Now, it's your turn."

You can use the same five steps to teach your child to identify his own boundaries by connecting with himself and communicating his boundaries in a respectful and loving way.

When setting your boundaries, keep in mind that a parent-child relationship is a two-way street. If you feel uncomfortable with your child yelling at you, he most likely also feels uncomfortable being yelled at. A fully connected parent-child relationship occurs when you are both respectful and willing to learn what each other's personal boundaries are and how to honor them.

Honoring Boundaries with Consistency

Confused, my clients often ask me, "Why is my child still testing my boundaries? I have had the same boundaries for years." One of the main reasons a child may not always honor his parents' boundaries, even after the parents explicitly communicate and teach them, is inconsistency in following through. When I ask my clients to begin paying close attention to their actions, they often find that there are times when they choose to avoid honoring their own boundaries, justifying it to themselves by being too tired, too busy, or not wanting to "ruin the day" because they know how their child might react. There are many other reasons why parents may choose to make an exception "just this one time."

The problem with inconsistency is that it creates confusion and uncertainty. For example, if a child interrupts his mother, and the mother, although feeling annoyed, chooses not to say anything, she teaches her child that it is alright to interrupt her. Next time he interrupts her, the mother decides to honor her boundaries and asks him not to interrupt her; she teaches him that it is not alright to interrupt her. Unwittingly, the mother confuses her child by sending him two opposite messages. Not knowing how his mother will respond to him interrupting her this time and hoping that this is a time when she will say nothing when he interrupts her, the child will continue interrupting his mother each time. The mother may get frustrated and even punish the child without realizing that, by being inconsistent, she taught him not to honor her boundaries.

In order to teach the child to honor her boundaries, the mother needs to honor them first by being consistent in following through on what she said she would do in response to the way her child interacts with her. If necessary, the mother could use the five steps to setting personal boundaries to reset them.

If you've had boundaries for a while, and your child is still what is commonly interpreted as "testing" them, it may be a sign that you have been inconsistent with your boundaries. There is no need to use it as a reason to beat yourself up or feel disappointed with yourself. Remind yourself that it's merely your primal brain trying to take care of you by protecting you from the emotional discomfort resulting from dealing with stressful situations.

You know that you are doing what's best for you and your child. If you need to, you can use the self-connection strategies from Chapter 7 to get in touch with yourself. From that connected place, you will be able to teach your child with encouragement, lots of love, patience, compassion, and even some fun while wholeheartedly believing in your child's ability to honor your boundaries consistently.

Boundaries vs. Punishment

Due to vague and often incorrect definitions of boundaries and punishment and contradictory information on the difference between the two in today's world, many parents mistakenly confuse boundaries with punishment. This confusion may result in unnecessary emotional suffering for the parent and child. Teaching a child to honor our personal boundaries is not the same as punishing the child.

While the purpose of teaching your child how to honor your boundaries is to help the child learn to treat you in the way you want to be treated, the purpose of punishment is to create circumstances that cause the child to feel strong unpleasant emotions, such as regret, shame, or guilt. By intentionally evoking unpleasant feelings in their child, parents hope that the emotional suffering will "teach the child the lesson," and the child will change his behavior.

The truth is that emotional suffering does not teach your child. You do. Imposing emotional suffering only harms the child's overall wellbeing and your relationship with your child. It doesn't take much to create the circumstances that evoke strong unpleasant emotions in your child; however, it rarely works the way parents hope it will. Besides, is that really what you want to do?

Even when the child does change his behavior based on strong negative emotions, his action does not come from a place of love but a place of fear. We cannot connect from a place of fear. Reconciling after the punishment may help the child feel better, but a lingering effect of emotional distress may remain in the child's heart or mind for a long time.

Unlike punishment, boundaries focus on *your* behavior versus forcing the child to change *his* behavior by imposing strong unpleasant feelings on him. You take responsibility for honoring your personal boundaries by letting the child know how you are going to honor your boundaries if he chooses not to and for helping him to learn to honor them successfully. It is also about teaching the child to honor your boundaries in a loving, respectful, and comprehensible way.

Here is a format you can use to communicate your boundaries: "When I'm treated this way, I feel this. If I continue to be treated this way, I will do this." For example, "When I'm being snapped at when I'm helping you with your homework, I feel unappreciated. If I continue to be snapped at, I will leave the room and wait until you are ready to talk to me in a respectful way." Phrased this way, it reminds the child what your boundary is and gives the child a chance to change his actions toward you.

A slight but very important nuance here is your tone of voice. Your tone of voice can turn even the kindliest and most lovingly intended boundary into a threat of punishment. When stating your boundary, make sure to use a calm, respectful, and neutral tone of voice to make it clear to the child that you are not threatening but informing him. Also, setting and honoring boundaries is not done in place of helping your child process his emotions. It's done either afterward or when you have observed your child's behavior enough to make sure that it is caused by his habitual way of behaving, not by his inexperience, confusion, or struggle to process his emotions.

How do you know whether you are teaching your child to honor your personal boundaries or punishing them? You determine it by connecting with yourself to become aware of how you feel. Because teaching your child to honor your personal boundaries comes from a place of love and care for yourself and the child, you feel loving and compassionate throughout the process. If you feel strong unpleasant emotions, such as anger, resentment, or contempt, you are coming from a place of fear and punishing your child. Setting your boundaries out of fear only leads to further weakening the connection between you and your child.

Boundaries and Connection

Having boundaries will allow you and your child to feel loved, respected, and connected. Setting and honoring boundaries does not have to be accompanied by strong unpleasant emotions and can be done in a respectful, calm, and loving manner. Remembering this will help you feel more at ease with this process. If you feel uncomfortable, remind yourself that emotional discomfort is optional and is not a reason to avoid setting and honoring your boundaries. You can change how you feel about setting and honoring boundaries by using the Parenting Success Formula and choosing to believe that having boundaries is essential if you want to establish a fully connected parent-child relationship.

Setting and honoring boundaries in healthy ways provides certainty and builds trust between you and your child. Having personal boundaries also helps you take care of yourself and feel self-connected, which allows you to be there for your child in a way that will help him feel even more connected to you. The more your child feels connected to you, the more amenable he will be to honoring your boundaries.

Connecting through Boundaries
Action Step

Continue to complete the exercises in your *Parenting Connection Workbook* to gain a deeper understanding of how you can implement and honor your boundaries.

AFTERWORD

The depth, joy, and strength of your parent child-relationship and its memories are not measured by your child's compliance, the opinions of others about your parenting, or the money spent on gifts for your child. It is measured by the meaningful connection between you and your child.

It has been my privilege to guide you on this journey. I trust that this book has helped you realize that you are already a parent who can give your child the foundation he needs—the fully connected parent-child relationship—to create the life he wants. Now you know that there is nothing wrong with you or your child; you are both worthy and lovable just the way you are.

In order to have a fully connected parent-child relationship, you and your child do not have to feel happy all the time. A parent-child relationship is not about happiness. Happiness is just an emotion that comes and goes. A parent-child relationship is about connection. Connection lasts a lifetime. When you feel connected, you can turn even the most unhappy moments into the moments that bring you and your child together, create pleasant and empowering feelings, and lead to lasting fulfillment.

By now, you have gained a deep understanding of your brain, your child's brain, and the needs of both of you. You have learned how to meet these needs in constructive ways that will help you and your child thrive and grow. You understand how to embrace and process your or your child's emotions instead of avoiding or resisting them. You know how to use those emotions to learn about and connect with yourself and your child. In addition, you have an effective tool —the Parenting Success Formula—that empowers you to use your brain consciously and purposefully in order to achieve the desired results.

Knowing and understanding something is good, but it won't make much difference in your life and your child's life if you do not practice it. Just like a child needs to practice eating with a spoon over and over again to master the skill, you will need to practice what you learned in order to internalize your new skills by rereading parts of the book, doing the exercises in the workbook, and consistently applying what you have learned. Just like your child, you will need to build new neural connections in your brain, which takes conscious and deliberate practice and repetition.

Although these skills take patience and persistence, they are invaluable beyond just your relationship with your child. Everything you have learned in this book can be applied to any relationship. When you know how to connect with yourself in a meaningful, profound way taught in this book, you will be able to connect with anyone else because we all want to feel loved, connected, and understood.

As you walk your journey of creating a fully connected parent-child relationship, remember to be compassionate, patient, and forgiving with yourself. It's not about being perfect. It's about looking at the mistakes you make along the way and asking yourself, "What can I learn from this?"

Your journey is about learning, celebrating each step, and moving forward. It's about using the challenges in parenting to get to know yourself and your child better. It's about using unpleasant emotions as signs that you may not be fully connecting with yourself and your child. It's about remembering that your child needs your love and connection with you as much as you do with him.

Now that you have what you need to create the parent-child relationship you and your child deserve, I encourage you to continue the rest of your journey. Many of my private coaching clients have successfully applied what they learned through our work together to transform their and their children's lives by creating the relationship they wanted to have with their child. If they did it, so can you. Connect with yourself and get started by putting your new learning into practice.

I want to thank you on my behalf and on behalf of your child for investing your time in learning and growing in your parenting.

As a lifelong learner, I am committed to constantly learning and growing to bring even more value into the lives of every family I work with. I love hearing from my clients and readers about how my approach has affected their relationships with their children. I would like to hear from you about what you have implemented from this book and how it worked for you. You can connect with me at albina@albinspire.com.

As you continue your parenting journey, know that I am always here for you. If you need a hand at any point, I am just one email away.

To your fully connected parent-child relationship,
    Albina Terpetska

ACKNOWLEDGMENTS

Just like it takes a village to raise a child, it takes a village to create a book. This book is a result of many people's contributions.

My deepest thanks and appreciation go to my best friends, coaches, and teachers who are always there for me—my mom, Svitlana, and my sister, Violetta, for everything they have taught me through their infinite love, perpetual patience, and unwavering support.

In addition to many other ways in which my loving and caring mom has enriched my life, she selflessly and generously gifted me one of the most valuable assets—time—at the cost of hers by running errands for me, cooking, and cleaning, so that I could focus on writing this book.

I am immensely grateful to my incredibly talented, insightful, and ever-supportive sister, whose constructive feedback, wise suggestions, and original ideas were invaluable in making this book possible.

A special word of thanks to my grandpa for his legacy— the priceless life lessons that will remain in my heart and mind for a lifetime and which I keep passing on to the families I work with.

Warm thanks to my "second voice," brilliant book editor Carly Carruthers, who was able to look at my work through the lens of both an editor and a parent. Carly's stimulating questions, enormously helpful feedback, and requests for clarification resulted in an even more valuable book.

I greatly appreciate Rory Carruthers, of Rory Carruthers Marketing, for his skilled help with book development.

My approach has been inspired by the works and lives of the extraordinary thinkers, including Nelson Mandela, Mahatma Gandhi, Mother Teresa, Martin Luther King Jr., Virginia Satir, Cloé Madanes, John Gottman, Daniel Goleman, Fred Rogers, Tony Robbins, John Grinder, Richard Bandler, Carol Dweck, Haim Ginott, Geneen Roth, Mark Goulston, Brooke Castillo, Adele Faber, Elaine Mazlish, Nathaniel Brandon, Doug Lemov, Milton Erickson, Viktor Frankl, Leo Gura, Maxwell Maltz, Daniel J. Siegel, Napoleon Hill, Brad Blanton, Byron Katie, Don Miguel Ruiz, George Leonard, Randy Pausch, James R. Doty, Stephen Covey, Travis Bradberry, Jean Greaves, James Allen, Walter Anderson, Dale Carnegie, Dorothea Brande, James M. Kouzes, Barry Posner, Joseph Grenny, Kerry Patterson, David Maxfield, Ron McMillan, Al Switzler, Susan Jeffers, and M. Scott Peck. I have learned from every single one of them, and I feel immense gratitude to them for the wisdom they have shared with us all.

Thank you also to my students who challenged me to find answers to the most complex and fundamental questions that adults struggle with when it comes to forming meaningful relationships with the children in their lives.

My heartfelt thanks to my school teachers and university professors who made an impact on my learning and teaching. I'm particularly grateful to my first teacher, Nadiya Tymofiivna Bezvuhliak, and university professor, Olena Vasylivna Zarichna, for being exemplary role models of a teacher and for helping me realize what a profound influence a teacher can have on a student.

I am grateful beyond words to the families I have been honored to work with who open their hearts and doors of their homes to me, share with me their most personal relationship challenges, and are a constant source of inspiration for me, for their courage and vulnerability. I have learned a lot from my experiences working with them.

And to you—for your relentless, persistent search for what you need to know to eliminate emotional suffering and create the parent-child relationship you and your child deserve. I hope that you will find all the answers in this book. You and your child are the reason I wrote it.

ABOUT ALBINA TERPETSKA

The creator of Albinspire Family Relationship Coaching, Albina Terpetska is a family relationship coach, an educator with a master's degree, and a licensed Neuro-Linguistic Programming Practitioner.

Albina has worked with hundreds of children of all ages and their parents for over seventeen years, empowering them to create the family they deserve.

Over the past decade, countless parents and children have benefited from working with Albina Terpetska by transforming their relationships and creating fulfilled and healthy families.

As an educator with a Master's of Education, family relationship coach, and licensed Neuro-Linguistic Programming Practitioner, Albina Terpetska has a deep understanding of human psychology, communication, and brain function. Based on the latest research, her own experience, and best practices, Albina has developed her profoundly effective, advanced, yet simple-to-implement approach and teaches it to parents and children in a well-structured and comprehensible way.

Having learned from the world's most successful experts through attending multiple courses, events, and online trainings, as well as mastering the areas of emotional intelligence, psychology, communication, and mindset, Albina helps families from diverse backgrounds achieve the results they want and create relationships they deserve, even in the most challenging situations.

In addition to parents, educators and caregivers also seek her advice. Albina coaches teachers by providing professional development training and modeling the best teaching and communication practices. These practices allow teachers of all grades to build rapport with their students.

As a life-long learner, Albina values professional and personal development. She is continuously researching, studying, and practicing the most effective, proven methods and principles in family coaching, child development, neuroscience, teaching, personal development, emotional intelligence, communication, mindset, and human psychology.

You can learn more about Albina's services at www.albinspire.com

NOTES

1. Why We Act the Way We Act

1. MacLean, Paul D. *The Triune Brain in Evolution: Role in Paleocerebral Functions*. Plenum Press, 1990.
2. Goleman, Daniel. *Emotional Intelligence: Why It Can Matter More than IQ.* Bantam Books, 2006.
3. Cannon, Walter B. *Bodily Changes in Pain, Hunger, Fear and Rage An Account of Recent Researches into the Function of Emotional Excitement*. McGrath, 1970.
4. Bandler, Richard. *Richard Bandler's Guie to Trance-formation:How to Harness the Power of Hypnosis to Ignite Effortless and Lasting Change*. Health Communications Inc., 2008.
5. Becoming More Fully Human with Virgina Satir, http://www.intuition-network.org/txt/satir2.htm.
6. "Giacomo Rizzolatti - Mirror Neurons." *GoCognitive*, gocognitive.net/interviews/giacomo-rizzolatti-mirror-neurons.
7. Rizzolatti, Giacomo. "Giacomo Rizzolatti." www.sfn.org>SfN>Volume-9> "HON_V9Rizzolatti"
8. Cerdán, Andrea García. "Mirror Neurons: The Most Powerful Tool. Learn Everything They Can Do." *Health, Brain and Neuroscience*, 7 Oct. 2019, blog.cognifit.com/mirror-neurons/.

2. How Your Child's Brain Works

1. Uytun, Merve Cikili. "Development Period of Prefrontal Cortex." *IntechOpen*, IntechOpen, 3 Oct. 2018, www.intechopen.com/books/prefrontal-cortex/development-period-of-prefrontal-cortex.
2. Buchsbaum, Monte S. "Frontal Cortex Function." *American Journal of Psychiatry*, vol. 161, no. 12, 2004, pp. 2178–2178., doi:10.1176/appi.ajp.161.12.2178.
3. "The Embryo Project Encyclopedia." Roger Sperry's Split Brain Experiments (1959–1968) | The Embryo Project Encyclopedia, embryo.asu.edu/pages/roger-sperrys-split-brain-experiments-1959-1968.
4. Siegel, Daniel J., and Bryson, Tina P. *The Whole-Brain Child: 12 Revolutionary Strategies to Nurture Your Child's Developing Mind*. Bantam Books, 2012.
5. Goleman, Daniel. *Emotional Intelligence*. Bantam Books, 2006.
6. Bradberry, Travis, and Jean Greaves. Emotional Intelligence 2.0. TalentSmart, 2009.
7. Donald Hebb Formulates the "Hebb Synapse" in Neuropsychological Theory: History of Information, www.historyofinformation.com/detail.php?entryid=4361.

8. "InBrief: The Science of Early Childhood Development." Center on the Developing Child at Harvard University, 27 July 2020, developingchild.harvard.edu/resources/inbrief-science-of-ecd/.

3. Your Child's Needs

1. Madanes Cloé. *Relationship Breakthrough: How to Create Outstanding Relationships in Every Area of Your Life*. Rodale, 2010.
2. Madanes Cloé. *Relationship Breakthrough: How to Create Outstanding Relationships in Every Area of Your Life*. Rodale, 2010.
3. Geisel, Theodor Seuss. *Horton Hears a Who!* Random House, 1954.
4. "Summit Medical Group Web Site." Summit Medical Group, www.summitmedicalgroup.com/library/pediatric_health/pa-hhgbeh_attention/.
5. Bogin, Barry. Patterns of Human Growth. Cambridge University, 1999.
6. Bogin, Barry. Patterns of Human Growth. Cambridge University, 1999.
7. Henry Dwight Chapin, "Family vs. Institution," Survey 55 (January 15, 1926):485-488.
8. "What History Tells Us About the Dangers of Separating Children from Parents." *PsychAlive*, 26 June 2018, www.psychalive.org/history-tells-us-dangers-separating-children-parents/.
9. *Adoption History: Henry Dwight Chapin, "Family vs. Institution,"* 1926, pages.uoregon.edu/adoption/archive/ChapinFvI.htm.
10. Sullivan, Erin. "Self-Actualization." *Encyclopædia Britannica*, Encyclopædia Britannica, Inc., 11 Sept. 2019, www.britannica.com/science/self-actualization.
11. Maslow, A.H. (1943). "A Theory of Human Motivation". In Psychological Review, 50 (4), 430-437.
12. Maslow, A.H. (1943). "A Theory of Human Motivation". In Psychological Review, 50 (4), 430-437.

4. What About Your Needs?

1. Madanes Cloé. *Relationship Breakthrough: How to Create Outstanding Relationships in Every Area of Your Life*. Rodale, 2010.

5. The Parenting Success Formula

1. Clear, James. *Atomic Habits: Tiny Changes, Remarkable Results: an Easy & Proven Way to Build Good Habits & Break Bad Ones*. United States, Penguin Random House, 2018.
2. Frankl, Viktor E.. Man's Search For Meaning. United Kingdom, Pocket Books, 1985.
3. Dalai Lama Center for Peace and Education. "Dan Siegel:Name it to Tame it." 8 Dec. 2014 YouTube. https://www.youtube.com/watch?

v=ZcDLzppD4Jc.

4. Siegel, Daniel J., and Bryson, Tina P. *The Whole-Brain Child: 12 Revolutionary Strategies to Nurture Your Child's Developing Mind*. United States, Bantam Books, 2012.

6. Transforming Your Beliefs

1. Greene, Ross W. *The Explosive Child: a New Approach for Understanding and Parenting Easily Frustrated, Chronically Inflexible Children*. Harper, 2014.
2. PhilosophieKanal. "Bertrand Russell - Message to Future Generations." *YouTube*. www.youtube.com/watch?v=ihaB8AFOhZo.
3. Denise Cummings-Clay, Hostos Community College. "Child Development." *Behavioral Psychology | Child Development*, courses.lumenlearning.com/atd-hostos-childdevelopment/chapter/behavioral-psychology/.
4. Dispenza, Joe. Evolve Your Brain: the Science of Changing Your Mind. Health Communications, 2009.
5. Rogers, Fred. *The World According to Mister Rogers: Important Things to Remember*. Hachette Books, 2019.
6. Roth, Geneen. *Feeding the Hungry Heart: the Experience of Compulsive Eating*. Plume, 2002.

7. Staying Self-Connected

1. Hoffeld, David. *The Science of Selling: Proven Strategies to Make Your Pitch, Influence Decisions, and Close the Deal*. TarcherPerigee, 2016.
2. Frankl, Viktor E.. Man's Search For Meaning. United Kingdom, Pocket Books, 1985.
3. Ruiz, Miguel. *The Four Agreements: a Practical Guide to Personal Freedom*. Amber-Allen Publishing, 2017.
4. Hendricks, Gay. *The Big Leap: Conquer Your Hidden Fear and Take Life to the Next Level*. HarperOne, 2010.
5. *Seven Practical Applications of NLP: How to Use NLP in Hypnosis, Business, Health, Coaching, Sport, Education and Public Speaking*. Attrakt, 2012.
6. Welch, Suzy. *10-10-10 - a Life-Transforming Idea*. Simon & Schuster Ltd, 2010.
7. Covey, Stephen R. The 7 Habits of Highly Effective People. Franklin Covey, 1998.

8. Helping Your Child Process Emotions

1. Covey, Stephen R., et al. *The 7 Habits of Highly Effective People: Powerful Lessons in Personal Change*. Simon & Schuster, 2020.
2. Goulston, Mark. *Just Listen: Discover the Secret to Getting through to Absolutely Anyone*. Amacom, 2015.
3. Bandler, Richard. *Get the Life You Want*. Harpercollins Publishers, 2009.

4. Roth, Gennen. *When Food is Food & Love is Love: A Step-by-Step Spiritual Program to Break Free from Emotional Eating.* Sounds True, 2006.

9. Connecting through Boundaries

1. Ida Soghomonian Posted September 23, 2019 within personal development. "Boundaries - Why Are They Important?" *The Resilience Centre*, 23 Sept. 2019, www.theresiliencecentre.com.au/boundaries-why-are-they-important/.

www.ingramcontent.com/pod-product-compliance
Lightning Source LLC
Chambersburg PA
CBHW022021090426
42739CB00006BA/229

* 9 7 8 1 9 4 9 6 9 6 1 4 1 *